Your home as your
best investment

HOUSERICH

HOWARDTURK

Prentice Hall Canada

A Pearson Company

Toronto

Canadian Cataloguing in Publication Data

Turk, Howard
    House rich : your home as your best investment

Includes index.
ISBN 0-13-064868-X

1. House buying—Canada. 2. House selling—Canada   I. Title.

HD1382.5.T86 2002   333.33'8   C2001-903678-7

ISBN 0-13-064868-X

Editorial Director, Trade Division: Andrea Crozier
Acquisitions Editor: Susan Folkins
Production Editor: Catherine Dorton
Substantive/Copy Editor: Lynne Missen
Proofreader: Mary Bitti
Art Direction: Mary Opper
Cover Design: Amy Harnden
Interior Design: Julia Hall
Author Photograph: Lorella Zanetti
Production Manager: Kathrine Pummell
Page Layout: Dave McKay

This publication contains the opinions and ideas of its author and is designed to provide useful advice in regard to the subject matter covered. The author and publisher are not engaged in rendering legal, accounting, or other professional services in this publication. This publication is not intended to provide a basis for action in particular circumstances without consideration by a competent professional. The author and publisher expressly disclaim any responsibility for any liability, loss, or risk, personal or otherwise, which is incurred as a consequence, directly or indirectly, of the use and application of any of the contents of this book.

ATTENTION: CORPORATIONS
Books are available at quantity discounts with bulk purchase for educational, business, or sales promotional use. For information, please email or write to: Pearson PTR Canada, Special Sales, PTR Division, 26 Prince Andrew Place, Don Mills, Ontario, M3C 2T8. Email ss.corp@pearsoned.com. Please supply: title of book, ISBN, quantity, how the book will be used, date needed.

Visit the Pearson PTR Canada Web site! Send us your comments, browse our catalogues, and more. **www.pearsonptr.ca**

1 2 3 4 5 WEB 06 05 04 03 02

Printed and bound in Canada.

A Pearson Company

*To my boys, Andrew, Alexander, and James, who have taught me
all about the "best" investment anyone can make.
You've always been my inspiration.*

Love, Dad

Contents

Acknowledgments

For me, writing is very much a learning experience. All learning experiences involve teachers in one form or another. The people I work with at First Canadian Title have taught me not only about real estate, but also about decency and the value of a common sense approach to business. I've never encountered a finer group of people; I am honoured to consider them my colleagues. Thank you to everyone at First Canadian Title for helping me along the way.

I am deeply indebted to Kiki Sauriol, who tirelessly researched some of the hard to find supporting facts used throughout *House Rich*.

As always, everyone I have dealt with at Prentice Hall Canada, as well as my ever-patient editor Lynne Missen, was a pleasure to work with. They must have a really good Human Resources department there, because without exception, they keep hiring great people!

The experts referred to in the final chapter are all busy people who graciously gave up some of their valuable time to share their unique insights. Special thanks to Peter Vukanovich (GE Capital), Moshe Milevsky (York University), Rick Lunny (TD Canada Trust), Peter Norman (Clayton Research), David Karas (Money Concepts), and John Kelly (Century 21). We are all the better off with your wisdom.

Last, but certainly not least, I thank my family for being so supportive of this project.

Introduction:
Your Home As Your
Best Investment

"My boy," he says, "always try to rub up against money, for if you rub up against money long enough, some of it may rub off on you."

— DAMON RUNYON

Like it or not, money rules our lives. Everyone worries about it to some extent, searching for rewarding financial advice. New theories constantly arise. Every season brings a new crop of gurus, each with his or her own recommended system of investment. And then when things don't work out, there really is not much more you can do than add their book to your garage-sale pile. How can you tell which investment option is best?

People often invest in things like stocks, whether through direct purchases or through holdings in vehicles like mutual funds, to fund their retirement. Yet the risk of being burned is real and the potential consequences severe. The stock market is volatile. For example, in the year 2000 alone, the Nasdaq plummeted in value by 39% — down a full 51% from its peak. If you had saved all your life, socking money away each and every month just like your advisers had recommended, hoping to retire in the year 2000, and if you had a significant amount of your money in stocks listed on the Nasdaq, you would be in a lot of trouble. You could have seen your retirement nest egg lose half its value! Sure, in the long run, share values inevitably rise — but that's little comfort when you have to buy groceries in the short run. You may not live long enough to realize the rewards of some "long-run" investing.

In reality, the classic investment options, such as the stock market, are so volatile as to freak out the best of us. Baby boomers are both working hard to earn money and inheriting money as their aging parents die off. The money lost in the markets very often cannot be replaced by earnings, and the inheritance is a one-time thing. This makes many investors gun-shy. When it comes to investments, you really have to ask yourself, "Am I feeling lucky?" If not, beware: markets are hugely volatile. Be sure you have the stomach for it before venturing forward.

On the other hand, while housing can be expensive, it has a way of going up in value. From a pure investment perspective, real estate is simply not as volatile as the stock market. Sure, real estate values can drop for a while, but the house value for you personally remains the same in that you are living there and obtaining satisfaction from that. Inevitably, values rise. When you think of housing in broad strokes, it's clear that the issues of investment strategy and home ownership are tied together. Housing is an investment and, for most people, their largest one. In fact, most people spend more on a house than on any other thing in their lives. There are some very good reasons to put your money into real estate, not necessarily as an alternative to stocks, but certainly as part of your overall investment plan. Real estate as an investment can perform very well — especially if done correctly.

One thing is certain. Everyone has to live somewhere. And more than just providing a roof over your head, your home is your haven, a safe place for you and your family to relax. It can be a way to express yourself creatively, designing your own living space and creating an aesthetically pleasing environment just for you. Your home is where you experience the joy of raising a family, watching your children's first steps, holding birthday parties, sharing the holidays, and more. For many people, life revolves around the home.

There are many perspectives on real estate as an investment. There are those who believe that housing is a great place to invest your money. After all, buying a house and paying a mortgage acts as a forced savings plan, a hedge against inflation, grows tax-free, and provides a personal living space from which you can derive great satisfaction. Others believe that real estate is nothing more than consumption, not much different than buying a refrigerator, something you need to have, but not the place for your money. I disagree. If you have to live somewhere anyway, why not approach real estate using some basic business principles, as well as lifestyle considerations?

Like any investment, however, home ownership is not without its risks. Vendors want to sell for as much as possible, realtors want to earn as much commission as they can, and renovation contractors try to sell you the sun and the moon. Where, when, and how you buy can dramatically influence the financial outcome of your investment. For the unaware consumer, this can be like walking into a minefield.

In fact, I've always been amazed at how intelligent people sometimes go into what seems like a state of amnesia when it comes to buying, selling, or owning their homes — abandoning sound business principles and falling for some of the oldest tricks in the book, which they know well. I have met smart business leaders who can be ruthless and aggressive in their business lives, yet allow themselves to be swayed by a salesperson pressuring them to buy or sell by creating a false sense of urgency to a situation ("If you don't buy now, someone else will" or "If you don't accept this offer, the buyers will go to the house down the street and buy it instead"). The result, almost always, was to their detriment financially.

It does not have to be that way.

Knowing the "ins and outs" of the whole process of buying, selling, and owning a home and treating it like the essential — and potentially lucrative — investment that it is can make all the difference to your pocketbook. Why not spend time learning tips that can maximize the financial benefit you can enjoy from buying, owning, or selling a home? *If you are going to spend money on a house anyway, why not spend it wisely?*

The simple truth is that there are things you can do that directly impact the financial outcome of your home ownership experience. Not bad, especially when the added bonus is a good roof over your head!

Abraham Lincoln once said, "If I had eight hours to chop down a tree, I'd spend six sharpening an ax." That's a powerful statement — and an important lesson about the value of preparation. When it comes to buying, selling, or owning a house, the point translates well. When buying a house, it's a good idea to learn whether or not to listen to the latest demographic theories, what type of house will likely appreciate beyond the average, negotiation strategies, best mortgage deals, how to deal with realtors, and so on. When owning a house, it's a good idea to understand what sort of renovations will add real value and generate a reasonable return based on its cost, and it helps to glean inside information from leading industry experts with various perspectives on how best to carry a mortgage and invest at the same time. When selling a house, it's a good idea to understand how even small things like the smell of fresh-baked bread can help sell your house, as well as gather pointers on how best to present your house to get the best deal possible.

That's what this book is all about: you, your money, your home, and common sense. It combines useful information on various issues relating to buying, owning, and selling a house with what seems like a rarity these days, namely, good old-fashioned financial common sense. Together, they can be combined into a powerful package.

Although you will likely spend more on a house than on any other single thing in your lifetime, you don't need to be house poor, putting all your money into a seemingly never-ending mortgage. If well planned, your largest investment can also be your best investment. You can become house rich!

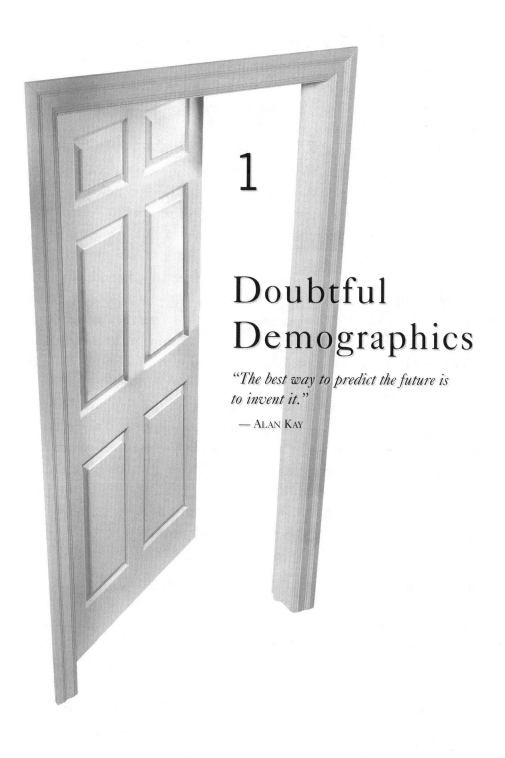

1

Doubtful Demographics

"The best way to predict the future is to invent it."

— ALAN KAY

Buying a home represents the single largest investment most Canadians will ever make. And with house value and mortgage rates so closely tied to the economy, and the economy itself so unpredictable, it's no small wonder that this purchase fills even the most seasoned real estate buyer with trepidation. So much is at stake. It would be nice to add certainty into what has always been a decision based on uncertainties. Who wouldn't want to know what the future has in store? Knowing what type of house to buy so as to increase the chances of getting big bucks down the line would be wonderful! When it comes to investments, everyone wants a crystal ball.

Forecasts of what the future holds for home values are wildly popular, particularly those dealing with demographics. Some of these demographic theories are simplistic and popular and some are complicated and quite technical, with analyses based on studies, graphs, and review of hard data. Some are right and some are just plain wrong — even if they sound nice.

This chapter reviews and discusses some of the popular theories and compares what they have predicted would happen to what has actually happened. It does not make a forecast but, rather, provides detailed information on what the trends actually have been. My goal is to provide you with the information necessary for you to make an educated decision based on hard facts on the issue of whether demographic-based theories should influence your investment decisions when it comes to home ownership. Having said that, remember that there is an element of luck involving educated guesses in all investments. Real estate is no different from other investments in this regard. The goal is to improve your odds.

The Real Estate Meltdown That Never Was

One of the most popular theories about real estate values was put forward by David Foot with Daniel Stoffman in their wildly successful book, *Boom, Bust & Echo*. The book makes for great reading, although when it comes to the real estate segment I think that there are some good reasons to doubt the accuracy of the conclusions. And many leading Canadian economists also disagree with Foot's conclusions.

Before we examine his arguments, let's consider what "boom," "bust," and "echo" refer to in Canadian society.

The "boom" relates to the growth in births between 1947 and 1966. In those years, the birth rate spiked, averaging 429,000 per year with a peak in 1959 of 479,000. That phenomenon was followed by a "bust" in the years 1967 to 1979, when the average birth rate per year dropped to 360,000, culminating in an all-time low of 343,000 in 1973 (clearly, not a good year for obstetricians!). Things changed again in the years 1980 to 1995 when the birth rate increased to an average of 382,000 per year, with a peak of 405,000 in 1990. That group — the children of the boomers — is called the "echo."[1] According to David Foot, "real estate is no longer a growth industry. That means it is a much better place to lose money than to make it . . ."[2] His advice to baby boomers is that they should not view their home as a pension plan. He goes on to say that even in the best neighbourhoods in the country, the days of large swift price increases are gone. According to Foot, "the real estate boom is over" and real estate values will drop because of the changing needs of the aging baby boomers.[3]

Foot based his opinions on demographics. In other words, Foot looked at the patterns of aging of our population (based in part on the data for birth rates) and drew conclusions from those patterns. According to him, there would be a real estate meltdown, in which the supply of housing would be greater than the demand in the period 2000 to 2010, causing a dramatic drop in real estate values.

The rationale behind Foot's theories lies in his views of the patterns of behaviour of each of the groups defined above. The premise is that people within a similar group will behave like one another. In Foot's view, people in their twenties typically leave their parents' home and enter the labour market. Within ten to fifteen years of doing that, those same people typically buy homes. Ten years after that, members of the "group" typically buy larger homes, renovate their existing home, or buy a cottage. Foot applied those clear factors to the housing market, using the known birth rates as a starting point. So, for example, if you look at the boom years (1947 to 1966) and added 20, then it would seem that in the years 1967 to 1986, a lot of people would be entering the labour market. Ten to fifteen years later, they should be buying houses and therefore there should be a boom in home values.

The problem, according to Foot, is that once those boomers are housed, the boom in real estate would end. The reason for this, in Foot's mind, is that the group following the boomers, namely the busters (born in the years 1967 to 1979), are, as a group, about 45% fewer than the baby boom group. Because the group is smaller, the demand they are able to create would also be smaller. If the demand for homes is smaller than previously, then prices should fall.

Finally, Foot contends that the echo group (1980 to 1995) will have an impact on prices once they reach buying age (when they are 30 to 35), except for areas from which baby boomers have moved away (such as leaving smaller centres in search of better jobs). That should happen around 2010. Because of that, Foot thinks prices for homes will increase after 2010.

To be fair, Foot does qualify his opinion. He does this in two ways. Firstly, he mentions in passing that there may be one last "mini-surge" in house prices before the 1990s are over. (Whatever a "mini-surge" is!) Making a prediction of a fall in real estate values while saying there may be an undefined mini surge sounds contradictory to me.

Secondly, Foot also indicates that factors other than demographics, like location of a property, the quality of the property, taxation of the property, and, lastly, economic cycles are important and do play "some" part in whether a real estate venture is successful. Well, of course they do! Yet Foot clearly says that two-thirds of long-term economic phenomena can be explained by demographics, so it's a bit unclear how important he really feels something like an economic cycle is to house values. Making a prediction of a fall in real estate values based on demographics and then saying, "Oh, by the way, there may be more to it," sounds contradictory and almost like a way of hedging one's bets. In my mind, this sort of "maybe this" and "maybe that" is a hint of the real truth — namely, that the issue really is not that clear-cut.

Foot's contentions certainly attracted a lot of media attention. They made for great press. The theory sounded so good, it must be true. Moreover, it all seemed so new and profound — and logical.

His ideas, however, are not novel. References to predictions of real estate values based on demographics (that time has also proven to be wrong) have been around in the U.S. for years. For example, as far back as in 1988, an American economist named Glenn H. Miller, Jr., wrote about the effect demographics would have on residential construction activities.[4] He predicted a decline in housing activity investments from 1986 to 2000.

Better known was a study done by two Harvard professors, David Weil and Gregory Mankiw, in 1989. The report was published in the *Journal of Regional Science and Urban Economics* with the title, "The Baby Boom, The Baby Bust, and The Housing Market."[5]

Weil and Mankiw essentially predict in their article that there would be a 47% drop in real housing prices between the years 1990 and 2007 due to the aging population. Their theory is that people's consumption of housing peaks at age 40 and drops thereafter. They believe that the number of households headed by someone over age 40 will increase while the number headed by someone under age 40 will decrease. If that happens, then demand inevitably either declines or does not grow as fast as it had done previously, resulting in falling values.

Weil and Mankiw are considered by many to be the founders of the "plummeting real estate value based on demographics" theory. Numerous academic reports have been written criticizing the Weil/Mankiw approach as flawed. Some experts, like those at the Canada Mortgage and Housing Corporation (CMHC), have stated that Weil and Mankiw are "incorrect" because they have confused the age effect and the group effect. Housing consumption actually does not peak at age 40 — it remains high up to age 70! Moreover, with the passage of so many years since the appearance of their article it's easy to determine whether or not they have been right or wrong. In fact, so far, the 47% drop in real housing prices between 1990 and 2007 has not proven to be correct. House prices are cyclical and the history has shown that while prices fell a bit between 1987 and 1993, they rose after that, and through the '90s. The market may be softening — but that has to do with an economic cycle, rather than a demographic one.

The bottom line is that popular predictors like Foot (and in their own way Weil and Mankiw) say that investment in a home will not be profitable. That's a bold statement. The question is, is it right?

No. The thing about the predictions found in *Boom, Bust & Echo* is that they don't refer to a scientific study or specific documented facts. Rather, they take easy-to-relate-to well-known facts and draw conclusions from them that are really nothing more than the author's thoughts. In my mind, they are really only proffering educated guesses. Demographic predictions of real estate values are typically wrong because demographics are only one part of the equation in figuring out why values rise or fall.

More Than Demographics

I believe that the soundness of the economy, low interest rates, low unemployment, immigration, and high consumer confidence have more to do with home values than merely how old the population is. And other experts agree. Dr. Frank Clayton (the principal of Clayton Research, a highly regarded real estate market consulting firm) thinks that Foot has confused a decline in the housing demand growth rate with a decline in overall demand. Moreover, Clayton says that Foot has overlooked important factors that affect house values, such as what is going on with the economy, changing number of households, and the emergence of non-traditional types of households such as adults living alone, singles, and couples without children.[6]

David Baxter (Executive Director of the Urban Futures Institute) agrees with the demographic data Foot uses, but disputes Foot's interpretation of that data. Baxter suggests that Foot's theories have created a "myth" relating to predictions of future real estate values, in that they offer simple explanations for a complex issue. He feels that Foot has taken something that is true and simple (a decline in the number of 25- to 34-year-olds in the future) and drawn false conclusions.

According to Baxter, it's true that the number of people aged 25 to 34 will decrease by 345,000 from 1996 to 2006, but it's also true that the number of people aged 15 to 24 will increase by 350,000 and that the number aged 35 to 44 will increase by 100,000. Moreover, the number of people aged 45 to 64 will increase by 2.5 million. Those are the people with the best possibility of owning a home. Baxter suggests that when boomers die, their children (a smaller group) will be at retirement age. What will maintain house values will be the growth in demand from the younger group, as well as what's left of the very sizable older group. He also feels that if immigration levels stay where they have been, there will then be no reduction in the foreseeable future in overall housing demand.[7]

The folks at CMHC also know a few things about house prices and the economy. In an exhaustive 1999 report,[8] Mario Fortin and Andre Leclerc examined Foot's contentions in an attempt to verify the validity of his arguments. In the summary of their 64-page report, they conclude, "The main factor that determines the long term change in real housing prices is the real income of the adult population."[9] According to CMHC's senior researcher, Ian Melzer, "What affects prices are factors like income, employment stability, maintenance costs, interest rates, taxes, immigration and migration between provinces. David Foot, for example, recognizes other factors, but he minimizes them." To this, I'd add the rate at which builders respond to increased or decreased demand by altering the housing supply. Oh, and by the way, CMHC says that "the real housing price is not likely to decrease in Canada over the course of the coming years."[10]

Even if you do rely on demographics, there is some sense that Foot has misinterpreted the numbers. For example, it's true that baby boomers represent the largest single age group in the country. But, it's also true that they gave birth to the second largest! In Canada, there are about 9.8 million boomers — certainly a large number. But, those boomers had about 8 million kids![11] If you look closely at the absolute numbers, you can see that the rate of retirement of boomers will be around 370,000 per year, starting about 2010, and that number will climb to about 425,000 per year in 2020.[12] An argument can be made that the boom-echo kids should pick up most of the slack, because they ought to be entering the market for houses at a rate of 360,000 to 400,000 per year for the next 25 years![13]

Another viewpoint comes from exploring the real impact immigration has on all of the numbers. That sounds obvious. How can all the people who come to Canada not have an impact on house values — after all, don't they buy houses too? In fact, immigration levels do have a lot to do with values in the real world. While it is true that demographics may be one of the factors that impact housing demand and that there may be some drop in some types of housing product or style demand strictly based on what boomers were buying, it may also be true that immigrants buying houses may compensate for that drop. Experts like Derek Holt of the Royal Bank think so. According to Holt, while it is true that the boom-echo kids will come close to replacing the demand of their parents for homes, there will still be a gap. However, that gap, or difference, "is likely to be more than made up for by immigration into Canada."[14] That's not hard to conceive. We have immigration levels of 200,000 to 250,000 per year and three out of every four immigrants are destined for the labour force (and consequently the housing market!). Think about that. Almost a quarter of a million people come here every year — it's inevitable that those numbers impact house values.

The Truth, the Whole Truth, and Nothing But the Truth

The facts speak for themselves. The actual housing numbers certainly do not support Foot's contentions (or those of the other demographic theorists). The real numbers reflect what others, like Dr. Frank Clayton, have been saying all along — namely, that good numbers come from a good economy.

Over the last few years, Canada has enjoyed relatively low interest rates, growing confidence by consumers, and a relatively low unemployment rate in historical terms. Add to that the beginnings of wealth transfer from boomers to their kids and it's no surprise that house prices have gone up.

That does not mean that prices will rise forever. Prices ride the roller coaster of economic changes.

Here is what has actually happened in Canada:

- Vancouver: house prices almost tripled in the last 20 years (Canadian Real Estate Association [CREA])
- Calgary: house prices increased fivefold in the last 27 years (CREA)
- Edmonton: house prices up 47% in the last 20 years (Edmonton Real Estate Board)
- Toronto: house prices up tenfold over the last 34 years (Toronto Real Estate Board [TREB])
- Ottawa: house prices up 153% over the last 20 years (CREA)
- Halifax: prices doubled in the last 20 years (CREA)

Here is some more of what *actually* has happened. The chart illustrates a clear trend in the time frame shown. Numbers like this are irrefutable — the picture they draw is crystal clear and flies in the face of Foot's myth.

Average Prices of Residential Properties in Canada

	2000	1999	1998	1997	1996
British Columbia	221,371	215,283	212,046	220,512	218,687
Alberta	146,258	139,621	132,905	124,865	117,673
Saskatchewan	94,047	91,396	87,577	83,978	77,478
Manitoba	87,884	84,525	86,419	85,404	85,318
Ontario	183,870	174,049	167,115	164,382	155,662
Quebec	111,260	107,501	103,947	101,715	98,435
New Brunswick	91,624	88,072	85,948	87,204	84,198
Nova Scotia	110,269	102,628	97,015	96,693	93,444
Prince Edward Island	82,884	82,138	79,577	86,403	83,922
Newfoundland	99,525	94,359	91,514	92,226	93,661
Yukon	124,756	120,723	108,537	100,141	87,054
Northwest Territories	144,948	149,515	155,441	149,628	158,300
CANADA	164,091	158,030	152,366	154,616	150,822

Source: Canadian Real Estate Association.

Oddly enough, none of this is really dramatic news for Canadians. In a recent Royal Bank survey,[15] 79% of Canadians believe that buying a home or condominium is a sound investment.

We are in an economy of low interest rates, consumers have high disposable incomes, the unemployment rate is low, and the rental markets are tight — even through ups and downs related to world news events (who could have predicted a war?). And that spells stability in the real estate market. Stability does not guarantee price increases. Rather, it means that prices will either rise or fall in a slow and steady fashion. Remember, prices always go in cycles. For example, looking back to the early 1980s, house prices were lowest in 1982 when interest rates were in the 22% range. As interest rates declined, house prices increased — peaking in 1988, then declining a bit until 1993, and rising again since then, with a slight decline in 2001. The cycles last years and have to do with prevailing economic times.

Other Popular Theories Based on Demographics

The idea of predicting real estate values based on shifts in spending patterns due to population aging takes many forms. One theory postulates that the owners of so-called "monster" homes will all sell when the kids grow up and leave, undermining the value of those houses. Other gurus believe that selling to fund retirement will impact real estate prices. As you can tell by now, I'm not a big fan of predictions based on demographics but think that these theories are worth discussing.

Selling "Monster" Homes When the Kids Leave

Advocates of this theory contend that when the baby boomers retire, they will trade their bigger homes for smaller ones. They will do this because their kids will have moved out, leaving them with unused and unwanted extra bedrooms. Aging boomers, apparently, will not want to maintain a large, empty house and will want smaller homes in the city closer to essential services, transportation, and entertainment. When this starts happening, there will be a surplus of big homes — especially of the so-called "monster" homes — on the market. If there are more monster homes than there are buyers (the next "group" being smaller), then prices will inevitably fall. Proponents of this theory suggest real estate is still a good investment — they simply caution that you should be careful what type of real estate you buy — and they believe that big homes in the suburbs are not desirable from an investment perspective. Moreover, if you already own a big or monster home, you are urged to sell before it's too late!

This theory might sound very plausible, but does it hold up under scrutiny? If the theory were right, then it would also be true to say that people live in the size of home that suits their needs. If that were true, then certainly as people's needs change, so would the types of homes they own. In other words, people who need smaller homes because their kids have grown up and moved out would typically live in smaller homes, and those with bigger families would live in bigger homes.

The numbers, however, show the opposite. Humans tend to spend upwards, towards the upper limit of what can be afforded. That is the psychology behind all luxury goods, and a home larger than one "needs" is nothing more than a luxury. Plainly put, people live in large homes because they can afford to indulge themselves, not really due to need. From this perspective, then, it's no small wonder that, according to a 1999 report issued by economist Derek Holt at the Royal Bank, incomes matter far more than the demographic dynamics of the family unit when it comes to the amount of living space that is desired."[16]

In his thorough report, Holt points to U.S. data, which he says is more comprehensive than Canadian. (He argues that this data can still be broadly applied to the Canadian market because both the U.S. and Canada experienced almost the same baby booms and have very close age distribution of population.) The U.S. data (from the U.S. Bureau of the Census) demonstrates that as family size has fallen over the last 25 years, the average size of the American home has grown (excluding a brief setback in the recession of the early 1980s). The shift pattern is clear — even as smaller households emerged (boomers moving out of their family homes), there was a clear preference for larger homes.

U.S. studies also examined why there was this preference and clearly show that there is a direct relation between the size of an average home and the income of that household.[17] Moreover, in the U.S., the percentage of people who were homeowners increased dramatically in the 1950s and 1960s — far too early for the boomers to have been the purchasers. The suggestion, again, from U.S. studies, is that the reason for that increase has to do with incomes, not demographics.

In the Canadian context, one would think that if the "monster" home theory worked, there would be few bedrooms empty since people would live in a home that suits their needs. In fact, a recent study by the Urban Futures Institute[18] showed that in the Greater Toronto Area alone, there were 533,740 empty bedrooms! Moreover, most of those homeowners have paid off their mortgages and, according to the study, will not move because of attachments to the community. Clearly, these numbers support Derek Holt's report and suggest that the U.S. numbers bear some correlation to the Canadian market.

Selling To Fund Retirement

This theory suggests that baby boomers will sell their large homes and move into smaller ones — or possible country homes — so that they can have money to live on in their retirement years.

It may be that those who advocate this theory rely on the clear data that shows that older people are less likely to own a home, and of those who do own a home, the home is likely to be smaller in size than what a typical person in their 40s and 50s would own.

The problem with this sort of thinking is that while the data is clear, the reason why is not. It may well be that the reason why the study showed older people being less likely to own a home than those in their 40s and 50s has more to do with when people of another generation entered into the housing market. It may be that older people tend to own smaller homes than people in their 40s and 50s simply because they bought homes a long time ago, when houses were built smaller. If these factors are true, then true doubt is cast on the theory of selling to fund retirement.

According to the Royal Bank's Derek Holt, "what counts more is how any trend in the home ownership of retirees might be changing. If they have been more and more likely to hold onto their homes decade after decade up to the present and if this continues into the future, that could suggest an ongoing behavioural shift that will continue to make it less likely to see mass selling."[19]

In fact, there is evidence supporting the notion of stable ownership. In the U.S., the rate of home ownership by retirees over the last 25 years has steadily increased! This may have to do with retirement income schemes, rising incomes, or just a shift in behaviour by retirees. For whatever reason, the trend is clear.

Things To Keep in Mind

Predictions of real estate values based on demographics are about as reliable as a carnival fortune teller. You need to know this in case you want to use these kinds of predictions as factors in whether or what to buy. It's just not a good idea.

- Do your homework. Look at what has actually happened and form your own conclusions.

- Remember that the popular theories do not always hold water. For example, David Foot contends that real estate is a better place to lose money than make it. Yet his conclusions have been challenged by housing experts.

- The soundness of the economy, low interest rates, low unemployment, immigration, and high consumer confidence have more to do with home values than merely how old the population is.

- We are in an economy in which interest rates are low, consumers have high disposable incomes, the unemployment rate, in historical terms, is relatively low, and the rental markets are tight — even through ups and downs related to world news events. And that spells stability in the real estate market.

- Other theories based on demographics, such as selling monster homes when the kids leave and selling to fund retirement, have also been proven to be untrue.

No one should make decisions in a vacuum, and for that reason alone, it's interesting to read the demographic theories. And they are not totally devoid of merit — they do raise issues that are worth considering. But take those theories with a grain of salt — time has disproved them.

2

Buy Smart

"Sure it's big enough, but look at the location."

— SHREK, FROM THE MOVIE, *SHREK* (UPON FIRST SEEING THE REMOTE CASTLE WHERE THE DRAGON HELD THE PRINCESS CAPTIVE)

B uying a house can be very tricky. There is a lot to know and the impact your choice has on your net worth can have a lot to do with how you go about buying in the first place. The reality is that some people will do better than others with their purchase. Some people know all the right moves — when and where to buy, what features are worth paying more for, the best way to use a realtor, and all the best strategies when it comes to real estate negotiation.

This chapter provides you with the essential information you need to become one of those people. It helps you to evaluate your options to get the best deal up front, as well as to maximize the long-term value of your investment. Buying a house is not simple. This chapter will help you buy smart.

Buy or Rent?

There's a lot at stake when you buy a house. Understandably, some people get cold feet and decide that they will rent, perhaps thinking that the money they possibly save per month could be invested and get a better return than they might get upon selling their house.

But let's look at the fascinating study Re/Max recently conducted,[1] which examined two investment options. The first option was to simply buy a home and live in it. The other option was to rent a two-bedroom apartment and use the money that would otherwise have been spent for the 25% down payment on the house, as well as any other savings, to invest in the Toronto Stock Exchange (TSE 300 Index), assuming that the renter would reinvest the investment dividends. The report also factored in ongoing rental and mortgage payments and considered the tax implications of the two options.

Re/Max looked at how house values have fared in various communities across Canada over the last 20 years, on average, as well as how the TSE 300 Index has fared in the same time period. So as to ensure that they were really comparing apples to apples, in both cases, the study assumed that the rate of growth over the past 20 years would continue for the next 25 years.

They then factored in what equity could be built in the house due to rising values as well as repayment of the mortgage principal. Homeowners came out on top! In most Canadian markets (except for Toronto where the TSE 300 Index and house prices rose at about the same rate), the TSE 300 Index has risen more rapidly than house prices. However, when you consider the actual dollars in and dollars out, *on an after-tax basis*, it is clear that buying a home is the better option. The following table outlines some of the study results in some major markets:

City	After Tax Value of Portfolio	Home Equity	Ownership Advantage
Toronto	$471,008	$1,040,393	$569,385
Vancouver	$795,536	$1,141,532	$345,996
Ottawa	$270,162	$505,758	$235,596
Calgary	$270,263	$399,230	$128,967
Edmonton	$185,728	$200,500	$14,773
Halifax	$328,114	$381,925	$53,811

Source: adapted from "Housing as an Investment," Re/Max, 2001.

Numbers can only reveal so much. Consider also that for most, living in an average home is nicer than living in an average two-bedroom apartment. Homeowners have a higher level of control over their living environment and better security about what their living costs are going to be. Remember also that for homeowners, the costs of running the household are greatest at the right time — when you are in your prime career years. As you pay off the mortgage, your housing costs decline at exactly the right time — when your income drops due to retirement or you have kids in university. The opposite is true for renters. They have a high housing cost right through their lives, regardless of their ability to pay.

Understanding Real Estate Markets

Okay. So having decided to buy a house, you might wonder, what's next? A good starting point is to understand that there are different types of real estate markets, namely, a buyer's market, a seller's market, and a balanced market. The type of market an area is in at any given time is the result of a variety of factors. One key factor is, obviously, the general state of the economy. In other words, when the economy is good, and the mood is optimistic, people tend to go shopping for things like cars and houses. When the economy is in a downturn, the reverse happens, and people tend to shy away from new long-term financial commitments. The economy has a direct relation to overall demand for homes at any given time. The level of demand is a key feature in what determines the sort of market at any given time. In an ideal world, you would buy in a buyer's market and sell in a seller's market. The trick, of course, is knowing when each market will happen. Economic cycles have a tendency to change without too much warning and, as a result, it's probably not a good idea to postpone a buying decision based solely on an expectation of a change in the type of market — predictors of what will happen with the economy are simply not reliable.

But markets do change — often very quickly — and they also have a frustrating habit of varying between neighbourhoods within any given city and even between streets in the same neighbourhood. There may be a buyer's market for one type of house and a seller's market for another type of house within the same city at the same time! For that reason, it is never a good idea to wait for the general regional market to change from buyer's to seller's or from seller's to buyer's. Rather, focus on the state of the market that affects precisely what you are looking for: the type of property in the location you desire.

Generally, though, over time, there are periods where real estate markets experience excess demand followed inevitably by periods of excess supply. These "swings" define market cycles. Real estate markets have a tendency to self-correct, in that when demand is greater than supply, prices rise. Those higher prices then decrease demand as well as inspire new construction — both of which allow the market to level and create a balance between supply and demand. How you negotiate and which strategies you adopt in the home-buying process have a lot to do with the type of market you are in. In other words, it's reasonable to consider the state of the market when deciding on things like the initial offer price, what conditions to insert or not to insert in the offer, and others.

Buyer's Market

A buyer's market is one where conditions are considered favourable to buyers. In a buyer's market, there is a greater supply of homes than there is demand for them. When this happens, prices tend to fall. From a buyer's point of view, this type of market is great — in part, because a buyer can take more time to shop. A buyer's market is considered to be a slow market. Because buyers may be few and far between, buying in this type of market can allow you all kinds of bargaining positions, which, in turn, translates to opportunity for a good deal, especially for first-time buyers, who are not burdened with having to sell one property in a down market in order to buy another. In a buyer's market, a buyer may be more likely to try to start the offer process with a low offer. Because buyers are scarce, the vendor may be more likely to try to work with the low offer and proceed by making a counter offer. The same rationale holds true for offers that contain many conditions. In a buyer's market, you are more likely to get away with a deal that contains conditions such as one making the entire transaction conditional upon selling your existing house.

Seller's Market

A seller's market is the reverse of a buyer's market. In a seller's market there are more buyers than there are homes for them to buy. That translates into a market of rising prices, since price is a function of supply and demand, and an inelastic supply, coupled with increased demand, makes for ideal seller conditions. If you are buying in this type of market, you may be faced with the spectre of having to compete with other offers on homes that you want to bid on. Moreover, it's likely that you may have to make some quick decisions, because someone else might be in line behind you to try to buy the same house. If you complicate your offer with too many conditions in this sort of market, the seller might just pass on your offer altogether and look to who is next in line. Most people want to try for a good deal when buying a home and start off with a low offer, but in a seller's market, that sort of strategy can backfire.

Balanced Market

A balanced market is almost a realtor utopia. The supply of homes available is just enough to meet the demands of those house-hunting. Reason prevails and prices are somewhat stable. Because of that, it's difficult to state whether or not the initial offer in this sort of market should be low or at the asking price. Anything can happen — the house you want can go cheap or may go beyond the asking price. The outcome in this sort of market has less to do with the state of the market as the needs and desires of the individuals buying and selling.

What Market Are You In?

Clearly, one bit of necessary information is what sort of market you are faced with. The best way to determine this is to ask a good realtor. They will know and should be able to guide you. And bear in mind that the state of the market in the region or city notwithstanding, it may be that the area you are interested in is "hot" and in demand. That means that it is possible for your city to be in a buyer's market overall, but that the neighbourhood you are interested in or the type of home you are looking for may be experiencing a seller's market — due to an aberration in demand. That can happen if the area has become desirable or trendy. Further, there can sometimes be a shortage of a certain type of property. When that happens, there can be a seller's market for that type of property until the supply increases to meet the demand.

Most often, this short-term phenomenon happens with properties like downtown condominiums. There may not be enough to meet a level of demand for a short while, creating a seller's market for the existing supply. New condominiums get built and the supply and demand equation becomes levelled, resulting in a shift in the type of market for that type of property. All this can happen quite independently of what is going on in that community for other types of properties. Remember, though, that in the long run, all housing products rise at a similar rate to one another within the same city or region.

Annual Season To Buy

It's commonly thought that buyers do well in the winter because not many people want to buy then and that sellers do well in the spring or summer because everybody goes shopping then. In fact, a recent poll showed that Canadians feel that December and January are the best times to buy a home and that April, May, and June are the best times to sell a home.[2]

While there may be a clear season for buying houses, that doesn't mean you have to trudge out in the snow to shop for a home. People sell their homes in all seasons. The best deal still remains the result of a variety of factors and can happen in any season. The reality is that in the winter, when buyers are supposed to do well, there is not as much selection as in the spring/summer because not as many people put their homes on the market, thinking they will not show well. Conversely, in the spring/summer, when sellers are supposed to do well, there is a lot of competition for the buyers because many other homes are then on the market.

The best bet is to work with a realtor. Ideally, when buying, you want to find a time when there is an imbalance in demand and supply (in other words a buyer's or a seller's market), so that you can make decisions armed with all the right information. Sometimes, blips appear for a short time in a community. It may well be that your community is enjoying a balanced market. It may also be, for example, that you want a detached bungalow and for some reason at the time you are looking there are more than the usual amount of bungalows out there for sale. The realtor will know that.

It's worth investigating the very local market in the area you seek. You want to know as much as possible before making any offer because it will likely affect the price you start with. If there are more detached bungalows available than usual, then you can probably start with a lower offer. The reverse is also true. If you want to buy a bungalow and the realtor tells you that they usually have ten to choose from at that particular time of year, but for some reason there are only three, you may want to consider waiting for the next season in that community (but never wait for a general regional trend from buyer's to seller's market). Either way, a good realtor will be plugged in and know what the local trends are in the area you seek. Some people prudently look to comparables in assessing what a good offer price should be. That's a great idea — but you need to be certain that the comparables are truly comparable. If you are not an expert and are trying to go solo, relying on the Internet, for example, then you need to be certain that you are really comparing apples to apples and not making an error by comparing apples to oranges. For example, if you are in the market for a three-bedroom detached house and the comparables you find are all four bedrooms, it may be a mistake to think that the extra bedroom has none or little impact upon the price of the house you seek. Or, it may be that you want an unrenovated "original" house and the comparables you find all have had varying degrees of renovation. In that case, it would be challenging for a non-professional to draw the right pricing conclusions from the comparables. A realtor can help you with this, since they are trained to understand comparables.

How To Buy Smart

Everyone wants to "buy smart." The question is, "What sort of house should you buy so as to get the most for your money down the road when it's time to sell?" Bear in mind that most people sell their house after five to seven years. Statistically speaking, the house that will appreciate the most must have features and attributes and be in a location that will be of appeal to the largest possible number of potential buyers, five to seven years from the time you buy.

Some housing "gurus" think they can predict what people will want in five to seven years, but I believe that the best way to figure out what future buyers will want is to look at what the trends have actually been and to apply some good old-fashioned common sense to the issue. Really, the best anyone can hope for is to be able to make an educated guess. Remember, investing does not come with any guarantees. But paying attention to the following factors can improve your chances of buying a property whose value will appreciate.

Location

If your goal is to get the most for your money (as opposed to buying a home that only meets your needs), then the location of the house is a critical factor. The location should be one that will appeal to as many potential buyers as possible down the road. One of the oldest sayings in the book for realtors is that in choosing a home, the three most important factors to consider are location, location, and location. Realtors are adamant about the importance of being careful in selecting a location. Ideally, you want to be able to best take advantage of whatever factors can make the home more valuable and minimize any of the downsides.

In evaluating a location, always consider what's going on with the economy in that area. A stable economy, with a diverse base, makes a region a place where people will always want to live — and that's important down the line. Take a look at community services. Are there good school and library systems? Is there any public transportation nearby? Is the current housing supply limited? These are all reasonable questions — and certainly factors to consider in selecting a place to live.

Some of these "lifestyle" factors can have a dramatic impact on your financial health. For example, in looking at the prospective investment value of a home, what you are really trying to do is get a glimpse of what the state of your future finances (in terms of net worth) will look like. If, for example, you find a house that is close enough to public transportation or to work so that you don't need a second car, then it's certainly worth taking that cost savings into account. Moreover, if you take the money you would have blown on the second car, invest it in an index fund, and leave it for seven years (about the average time people own a given home), you may find in the end that your overall net worth has increased more than what the house's value has increased (depending on the stylishness of the area and the overall market). You may be well advised to take the saved money and pay down your mortgage — since mortgage payments are not ordinarily tax deductible. Factors that save you money can be just as important as factors that make you money! (See Chapter 7 for a more thorough discussion.)

A low crime rate and fair taxes are also factors that make an area desirable. While there is no guarantee that seven years later, the same will hold true, it's also fair to say that having those advantages now may increase the chances of the area having those advantages in seven years.

After considering the area as a whole, it's wise to take a close look at the immediate surroundings. The houses in the neighbourhood should be similar in size and feel. You don't want to buy the biggest house in an ordinary neighbourhood because the surrounding smaller ones will drag down its value. For example, a four-thousand-square-foot four-bedroom house is best purchased in a neighbourhood where that type of house is common and not where all the other houses are three-thousand-square-feet three-bedroom houses. On the other hand, you may be well advised to spend the same money on a house smaller than the surrounding ones, but in a better neighbourhood, because the larger houses tend to drag value upwards. If you buy the largest house on the block, then the price you pay should reflect that it's not in an area of similar houses. (In other words, you should pay a lower price.) The house should not be worth what another large house in an area of large houses would be, unless there is something unique about the location, in comparison with the area of large houses. The problem is that when you sell, you are still in the market for that neighbourhood. You are better off getting a smaller house but on a better street because at selling time, the location typically is a major driving factor and you will either be more likely to sell it faster or benefit from a greater rise in prices that a "more desirable" neighbourhood typically enjoys.

Next, consider where the house is in the neighbourhood. It's better to select a house that is close to the middle of the neighbourhood than one at the edge. Avoid locations that back onto busy streets and those where your street acts as a traffic shortcut. Corner lots attract more street traffic and are not as safe for children and should also be avoided. Some ethnic groups have principles such as feng shui that dictate desirable and undesirable features in terms of location of a house on a street. These may be worth paying attention to — especially if you feel that those factors are likely to influence prospective purchasers when you are ready to sell.

Lastly, it's a good idea to look at your immediate neighbours to see how well they maintain their properties (if the neighbouring properties are rundown, it can negatively impact your property value). Also, check out the noise level (day and night) and find out what local utility charges are.

The "Buy Smart" House Features

In the U.S. (U.S. trends are very similar to Canadian trends, since basic American needs and wants are much the same as ours), the National Association of Home Builders recently conducted an exhaustive survey.[3] Here's what they found.

- 20 years ago, 25% of homes had four bedrooms.

- 10 years ago, 36% of homes had four bedrooms. (Note the upwards trend.)

- 20 years ago, 15% of homes had two bathrooms.

- Today, 50% of homes have two bathrooms. (Note the upwards trend.)

- The average house size in 1970 was 1,520 square feet.

- The average house size today is about 2,200 square feet. (Note the upwards trend.)

The same study found that almost 66% of new homes have a fireplace and that 81% have air conditioning. Kitchens are important: buyers like the idea of being able to see into the family room from the kitchen and also prefer kitchens with islands, room for more than one person to cook, walk-in pantries, and big windows. Most buyers would rather have parks and walkways nearby than fitness centres or pools. People seem to like higher ceilings, extra storage space, easy-to-reach laundry rooms, a formal dining room, and one big room instead of separate family and living rooms. Aging boomers value main bedrooms on a main floor. Lastly, an emerging trend for builders is to build homes with wiring capable of handling future Internet needs.

An interesting side note is the trend to do away with formal living rooms. More than half of the buyers surveyed said that they would rather have a larger family room, but no living room. This only makes sense. Very often, the living room only gets used a few times per year, such as at family gatherings for holidays. Even then, a lot of people still spend time in the kitchen or family room since that's where all the action is. (Ever notice where people gather at parties? The kitchen is usually the room jammed full, while the living room sits tidy and empty.) Many people feel they are better off spending their money on the space that gets used every day, rather than on space that hardly gets used. In fact, a leading U.S. expert recently predicted that within the next 5 to 10 years, the average home would no longer have a living room.

It's essential to beware of "unique" features. For example, you might be a young couple with no kids (DINKS — "double income no kids") and find a beautiful home in a family neighbourhood with a huge master bedroom with walk-in closets and dressing areas. The house would be perfect for your needs at the time of purchase. I know someone who bought a house like that. They had no kids and the house was perfect for their needs (huge bedroom, beautiful ground-floor entertaining area, the works). They grabbed it! A few years went by and they had one child. Fortunately, the house did have an extra small room and the kid went in there. Then, they had another and problems arose. Suddenly the huge bedroom and walk-in closets and dressing areas seemed like a waste of space since there was nowhere to put the second child. No problem, they thought. We'll sell and buy another home. They tried to sell, but found that no one wanted a huge house in a prime neighbourhood with only two bedrooms. With no takers, they were forced to renovate and restore the home to its original design — a four-bedroom home in a neighbourhood of four-bedroom homes.

Granted, this is an extreme example. The moral of the story, of course, is to try to buy a house that will suit your needs into the longer term and be of appeal to a wide audience of future homebuyers.

The trends mean that most people want homes with more bathrooms, more bedrooms, and more square footage. So when you select a house, you should place importance on the number of bathrooms and bedrooms; the house you buy should have as many of the desirable features as possible. That's buying smart. Not having a living room, but having a larger family room means that the home is consistent with the established trends.

By way of counterpoint, there are those who think that the market will shift towards smaller homes. Will Dunning, a leading Canadian economist and housing industry expert, believes that the market for larger homes is changing. He says the market for three-thousand-square-foot homes in the suburbs is the "softest" part of the market. He feels that young people cannot afford bigger homes and that with children moving away from home, older people will be "disillusioned" with all the trouble of running a larger household.[4] I'm not sure I agree (see Chapter 1), but I do think there is some merit to the notion that many people just entering the market want smaller homes like townhouses or condominiums so that they can be closer to work and to city services.

Newly Built Homes and Selecting Upgrades

People buying newly built homes from builders are also well-advised to consider future saleability in selecting upgrades. They too should "buy smart."

There are two general rules of thumb in dealing with the issue of which upgrades to choose. The first is that you should choose upgrades that are functional or useful as opposed to ones that are only decorative or aesthetically pleasing. The second rule is that you should choose ordinary features or styles that are of wide appeal as opposed to things that are bizarre or unusual. Select upgrades that would appeal to almost anyone who might be buying your house. For example, finishing a basement is a good upgrade. It's functional, because it adds more usable space. Almost anyone who buys that house will find the upgrade to be a thing of value. The same may not be true for deep pink walls and carpet — which may be of appeal to only a limited number of buyers. Most people would not pay more for that sort of upgrade.

Other functional upgrades that almost always make sense from an investment perspective are the first fireplace (any beyond that don't pack as big a punch), as well as kitchen upgrades such as better cabinets, a gas stove, or hardwood flooring. Consider the colour of the hardwood floor. If you stain it too light or too dark a colour, you limit its appeal to future buyers and may undermine the wise choice of selecting that form of upgrade in the first place.

Overall, you should be leery of falling into the trap of overdoing it with upgrades. When it comes time to sell, buyers will look at your house in comparison to the others in the neighbourhood. If yours is more expensive than all others because you are trying to recoup the cost of a lot of upgrades, you may find yourself sitting with a very hard sell. People will pay more for reasonable upgrades that appeal to them, but will typically not pay 40% or 50% more. From the buyer's perspective, they may be better off buying the house with fewer upgrades — and, hence, paying less — and then gradually adding what they really need and want on their own.

Lastly, there is an intangible element to all this. If you do go wild with the upgrades, there is a lifestyle value to having them: you will enjoy them and derive satisfaction in owning a house with them. And from a strict monetary view (which is what this chapter is really about), while you may not get that much more for your house, you will likely have a house that will sell faster than others because it is more appealing. That saves money and carrying costs and is bound to lower anyone's anxiety level — and there is certainly value in that!

Looking at Real Estate Trends

It would be great to be able to say that studies show that a certain type of house in a certain type of neighbourhood will appreciate more rapidly than the average. The reality is that there is not sufficient consistency nationally in any of the tracked trends to form a conclusion that a certain type of house in a certain type of neighbourhood will always be more likely to increase in value at a rate greater than the national average. The numbers just don't work that way. The trends do, however, indicate a few things:

Certain Age Groups Like Certain Types of Homes

Generally speaking, very young and very old people (who typically have less money and need less space) will choose homes that require less maintenance, such as semi-detached or apartment-type homes, which may share a driveway (less snow to shovel) and have a common roof (fewer eaves to clean), among other things. Couples will typically choose single-family houses. Most people in a city like Toronto — or any other urban area — want to buy detached homes in established neighbourhoods.[5]

What this means to you: If you believe that there will be a trend for the aging population to sell their monster homes and buy smaller ones, then you may want to buy a smaller residence with less maintenance, if only to wait for its value to rise.

Local Trends Tend To Be Short-Lived

Sometimes a type of building will suddenly take off in popularity. Condos, for example, may rise in price in the short run, if the demand where you live exceeds the supply. That's great to be able to capitalize on — but only if you can buy just when the equation is out of balance. What happens, though, is that builders see the demand and build (actually, they sometimes overbuild) to fill the demand, which eventually levels off the price rise. Builders are a sort of equalizer, balancing out supply and demand with new housing stock as necessary. All types of real estate investments rise in the long run.

What this means to you: The good news is that you will likely make money no matter where you buy. The better news is that local trends do exist — and if you can catch a trend on the way up, it is possible to outperform the market in general.

Lifestyle Communities Are Newly Popular

In Canada's bigger cities, aging boomers seem to like the idea of a vacation community that is close to the city. "Lifestyle communities" are a new kind of development sprouting up around the perimeters of the cities. It's anyone's guess as to what the capacity is of the market. The first builders to build these communities will, no doubt, do well, and the first buyers will likely see value increases (for a while) until other builders jump in and build more to meet demand. Prices are a function of supply and demand — and because the supply of houses is not fixed (they keep building more), it's difficult to predict future values.

What this means to you: If you are approaching retirement and find this sort of community appealing, buying now may be a great short-term investment.

Prices Increase in Different Parts of the Country at Different Rates

Take a random time period sample of January 2000 to January 2001. In that time period, the number of house sales increased by 40% in Ottawa, but declined 9% in St. John's. Vancouver had a 23% increase, but Regina had a mere 3% increase.[6]

Additionally, if you look at the average resale house price and compare the percent change year over year in different communities, the variance in the increase among the various communities is remarkable. For example, in 2000 the national average resale house price went up by about 4%. Yet, if you were fortunate enough to be in Nova Scotia, your home went up by 7.7%! Fellow Maritimers in PEI also had a price increase — but of only 1%! A few years before that, in 1996, the Nova Scotia average resale house price went up by 4.1%, yet the Islanders (PEI) enjoyed a price increase of 13.7%![7]

Even looking at numbers for different types of houses does not provide much guidance. For example, compare the results year over year for the first three months of 2001 to the first three months of 2000, as Royal Lepage recently did. Their study shows that in that period, in the markets they looked at (most of Canada), 85.3% of detached bungalows and 83.5% of standard two-storey houses went up in value, while only 74.1% of condominiums had such luck.[8] Reading that, you might think that detached bungalows are the things to buy, since more of those went up in value than any other type of home. However, the study also showed that the average price for standard condos went up 6.7%, while the average price for the standard two-storey house went up 6.3%. The house that looked the best from the first set of numbers — detached bungalows — only rose 4.3%! The condos rose at a pace faster than the detached two-storeys or bungalows.

Yet, to add more fuel to the fire, a recent CMHC study[9] showed that only about 16% of those who intend to buy a home intend to buy a condominium — the rest would prefer detached houses. That's confusing. Moreover, that same study showed that almost 40% of those who intend to buy want to buy a newly built house, yet sales of newly built homes are not anywhere near that number!

What this means to you: The numbers vary, making it difficult to buy as a money-making venture based strictly on overall historical trends.

Values Rise at Different Rates Even Within the Same City

Even if you look within one given city, prices are still all over the map. In Toronto, for example, it's interesting to compare what has happened to home values in different parts of the city.

Houses in Wards 14, 20, and 22 saw values go up by 35%, 32%, and 35%, respectively, between 1996 and 1999. In that same time frame, houses across town, in Wards, 39, 40, and 41, saw meagre increases of 6%, 8%, and 6% — nothing to write home about, especially considering inflation.[10]

There are a variey of reasons why there might have been such a big difference in the increase among the neighbourhoods. Ward 14 is Parkdale–High Park. That area has a combination of older affluent neighbourhoods, as well as seedier parts that are being renovated and cleaned up. It's an up-and-coming area and stylish. Wards 20 and 22 are largely located within Toronto's exclusive Forest Hill area. That area has traditionally been the home to some of Canada's richest citizens and has always been desirable. Wards 39, 40, and 41 are all located in Scarborough. That neighbourhood is clearly not one that people aspire to live in, being considered urban sprawl.

What this means to you: House values have been somewhat volatile over the last 20 years. Where you live within a city can make a big difference. Some areas will appreciate more than their neighbouring areas within the same city. There are opportunities for short-term gains.

What Can We Learn from Trends?

Why did the trendy and affluent area enjoy increases and why did the prices, after adjusting for inflation, go down in Scarborough? How does this lesson help prospective homeowners choose where to live? The answers provide some valuable insight for homebuyers.

In the long run, prices will rise more or less at an even level across most of the country, regardless of the type of house and the area. Prices rise more quickly in certain areas because those areas become more in demand, largely, in my opinion, due to issues of style. In other words, certain areas become trendy and popular. When that happens, demand increases and prices inevitably rise. A good example of this is Toronto's Annex area, where prices have risen over 40% in the past two years. The area has become stylish. People want to live there and, as a result, prices have gone up. In fact, prices have gone up a lot, and it may be that they have peaked — meaning that from an investment perspective, buying in the Annex may no longer be a good idea. Of course, if you think prices there have not gone up all they might, then buying there makes good sense. It's all in how you perceive the style trend to be.

The risk, of course, in buying into any area where prices have risen faster than average for the region is that the area may be mispriced — the prices do not reflect the fundamental demand.

Toronto's Forest Hill is also stylish, but is probably less likely to decline in value, for a number of reasons. Forest Hill is in the middle of the city. As the city grows, the value of being located centrally, close to services, shopping, and entertainment, goes up. Regardless of the state of the economy, there will always be a small group who have done well financially, who place value on living in a "stylish" area, and can afford the luxury of paying a lot of money for a home that is in Forest Hill.

Parkdale–High Park has also become desirable. The older, rundown Parkdale houses are being renovated or torn down and converted into desirable residences with good access to downtown. It's a matter of style. Parkdale–High Park has become trendy — people want to live there because other people want to live there and it's considered to be a cool area.

Scarborough, on the other hand, is not known locally as being the sort of place where stylish people would want to live. Physically, both Scarborough and Parkdale–High Park have similarities. Both are about the same distance from downtown Toronto as one another. Both have good highway access to the city core (Parkdale–High Park has the QEW, while Scarborough has the 401/DVP). Both have big shopping malls nearby (Parkdale–High Park has Sherway Gardens and Scarborough has the Scarborough Town Centre). Yet Scarborough is not considered as prestigious as living in High Park or even (these days) Parkdale. In my opinion, style is the determining factor.

The fact that stylish neighbourhoods appreciate at a rate higher than average means that there is an opportunity for short-term monetary gain by buying in areas that have either just become stylish or which are about to become stylish. The short run for house values can prove to be very interesting and is worth looking into, especially if you are planning on buying a house more frequently than most people do. In the short run, the stylishness of the area makes a huge difference. However, buying a house in a certain area only because you feel it will appreciate in value (higher than the average) carries some level of risk. For example, the next "hot" area may currently be a bit rundown and have a high crime rate. From a monetary perspective, it may make sense to buy there before the trend rises — since you would be in on the ground floor of an up-and-coming area. From a practical perspective, though, you might wind up raising your children in the company of people you might not really want them associating with. Generally, you should keep prospective value in mind, but it should not be your sole consideration.

How can you tell if an area has just become stylish? The best way to figure out what has happened to the type of home you want in the area you desire is to speak to a local realtor. A good realtor will know what has happened in the area in which you are looking. They should also know of anything unusual that is about to happen to the neighbourhood (like a new shopping mall or half-way housing for paroled criminals) that might have an impact on prices after you close. If you have Internet access, another option is to look at the data Royal Lepage offers on its Web site (**www.royallepage.ca**). One of the features the site offers is the "neighbourhood price trend calculator." Using this calculator, you can quickly get an idea of what has happened to the value of the type of home you are looking for in your specific area. Anyone buying a resale home in Canada these days should take a look at that feature.

Trends can be confusing and contrary. What happened in the past can suddenly be turned on its head. One thing is quite clear, however, in analyzing Canadian markets: in the long run, based on what has happened so far, it doesn't matter much where and what you buy — it all tends to go up or down with the state of the real estate market. Of course, it's worth keeping in mind the age-old classic economics theory about short versus long-run planning. That theory simply states that in the long run — we're all dead!

The Problem House

In the "buy smart" hunt, you may encounter the "problem house." Problem houses, which are commonly referred to as "fixer uppers," have something unusual about them and usually require lots of work. However, you may have been looking for a while and have not been able to find exactly what you want. Of what you have seen, the rooms may not have the right configuration or even if they do, you may not want to pay for the décor that you don't really like. You may want to consider buying a "fixer upper." These types of houses do not have mass appeal. Many people cannot picture how the house will look once renovated, and many simply will not have the stomach to deal with all the nonsense that goes with working with renovators and contractors.

However, if you do have a good eye for what can be, and if you are willing to duel it out with renovators, then buying a house that needs a lot of work may be a great opportunity.

From an investment perspective you need to look carefully at this sort of house. Find out what's really wrong with it. For example, if it's been languishing on the market and needs a lot of work, but is on a busy street — then you need to consider that no amount of renovating will change the location. Money invested here may be a waste because of a problem you cannot fix.

If you do find a "fixer upper," then find the answers to these questions:

- How much will it cost to renovate? (Be sure to add at least 10% to what the contractors tell you — one of their favourite scams is to omit things and then charge you for them as "extras.")

- How much will the house be worth when finished? Your realtor should be able to show you similar homes in the area that are finished.

- How much will it cost you to live while the renovations are going on? Factor in carrying costs and living expenses — you may be unable to live in the house during the renovation.

In the end, the finished value should be greater than the sum total of the purchase price plus renovation expense, less carrying costs. If it's not, then strictly from an investment view, you shouldn't go forward. This, of course, does not consider the lifestyle value of having exactly what you want. Bear in mind that the issues faced by new homebuyers in selecting upgrades apply here too. As I've said before, you don't want to have the most expensive or overdone house on the street.

Sometimes you find a house, make an offer but don't get it. Later on you discover that the house is back on the market! The reality is that not all deals close. The house sale may not have closed for any number of reasons. Most often, the house does not close because the buyer got "cold feet" (because they lost a bundle in the stock market or lost their job, etc.) or because of some defect with the house that the buyer was not willing to accept.

If you are still interested in the house, you need to get to the bottom of what happened. It may well be that there is nothing wrong with the house. However, it does happen that houses that are listed, sold, and then put back on the market often pick up a bit of a stigma, and that stigma (which is short term in nature) may be an opportunity for the buyer. Houses like that tend not to do as well the second time around. It's hard to get realtors excited about an "old" listing, and most people look first to new listings.

If there is a problem that relates to the actual house, get a home inspection (or do your own) and negotiate with the repair costs in mind. If there is really nothing wrong with the house but the first deal just fell apart, then the seller might be more amenable to a lower price — making this house a potential good deal. Do your homework!

Realtors

Never before have buyers been faced with so many options in their hunt. Should you use a realtor or just look yourself? Can you get a better deal by hunting without an agent? What are the pitfalls and risks in buying an FSBO (For Sale By Owner)? Should you sign a buyer agency agreement?

What is the best way to find a realtor and when you do find one, how do you know if he or she is any good? These are all perfectly reasonable questions.

For starters, let's look at how buyers find agents much of the time. You may be reading the paper or scanning the Internet and see a house that's being advertised or you may have driven down the street and saw a house with a For Sale sign that caught your interest. Either way, you pick up the phone and call the realtor who advertised the listed house. You make an appointment to view the house and, at the appointment, you have an opportunity to meet the realtor directly. For some reason, the house is not right for you. The realtor's next question to you (and they do this only about 100% of the time) is, "Can I show you something else?" If you say yes, chances are that's the realtor you will work with from here forward. Realtors, of course, know that this happens and it may well be one of the reasons they advertise a house and have open houses: to foster new clients. Selecting a realtor at an open house may not be the best thing to do, however.

This scenario is very typical. The surprising reality is that most buyers do not invest nearly as much energy in finding the right realtor as sellers do (see Chapter 3).

There are three basic types of agents. A "listing agent" is just that — one who takes listings, places them on the Multiple Listing Service (MLS), and deals mostly with sellers. A "buyer's agent" is a realtor who does the opposite, acting for buyers. They have knowledge of what is generally for sale (and also scan the MLS for suitable possibilities) and are accustomed to dealing with buyers, as opposed to sellers, and meeting their needs. The third is a hybrid — one who acts for whomever they can.

Let's go back to the story. Suppose you like the house that you saw the ad for and viewed with the listing agent. You have no agent so you ask the listing agent to draw up an offer. The agent asks you what price to put in and you name a number. You then add that the price you are offering is merely a starting point and not your final offer. In fact, you sheepishly admit, you are really prepared to go up another $10,000. Guess what? The agent has an obligation to tell that to the sellers! That's because the agent has a higher fiduciary duty to the seller than to you. The agent is not "your" agent — even though you may think he or she is. That agent is the seller's agent. If the seller asks the agent whether the number in the offer is as high as the agent thinks you will go, he or she has to tell the truth.

A good question, then, is why not get your own agent? In fact, that's exactly what you should do: retain a buyer's agent. Then sign a buyer agency agreement, which clarifies who is responsible for what and defines the fiduciary obligations of the agent to the buyer. While there are strong reasons why a buyer should sign a buyer agency agreement, note that the agreement is also a benefit to the realtor. Put yourself in the realtor's shoes. You invest a lot of time and effort in researching the right house for clients, driving the clients around town showing them houses, and then one day on a Sunday walk, the clients waltz into an open house, fall in love with the place, and then buy it — *without the agent*. The agent, of course, can kiss his or her investment in time and energy goodbye.

A buyer agency agreement obligates the buyer to work with the realtor they engaged. The contract should be for a specific time frame and must have some cancellation provisions. Some buyers limit the contract to homes that are listed on the MLS, thereby allowing them to buy a FSBO (For Sale By Owner).

The best way to find a good buyer's agent is getting a reference from someone you know who has had successful dealings with the agent, especially in the same neighbourhood you are contemplating buying in. If, however, you do not know anyone who has used a buyer's agent in the area you want, the next best thing is to ask those who deal with all the agents. A safe bet is your local real estate lawyer and local lender. In order to do what they do, they must, by necessity, come across a multitude of agents. They are in a unique position to know who is good and who is not.

In interviewing the buyer's agent, consider the following:

- Does the agent know right off about houses that are available that might suit your needs or does he or she have to go back to the computer to research? The agent should have a passing familiarity with what is available and be able to tell you whether or not your expectations are reasonable.

- Does the agent ask you questions? One way to tell whether or not the agent is on the ball is if he or she asks you questions about your finances (in order to know how much you can spend and what price range of houses to show you) and about your needs and expectations (in order to know whether you can really afford what you want).

You want an agent who will not waste your time telling you what you want to hear, an agent who will be brutally honest with you and tell it to you straight.

The Perfect Agent

A recent study looked at the five most important attributes people want in a real estate agent and then asked the respondents to identify a celebrity or historical figure that best exemplified that attribute.[11] The survey showed that the perfect agent would possess the experience of someone like Margaret Thatcher, the integrity of Abraham Lincoln, the intelligence of Albert Einstein, be as hard-working as Mother Theresa, negotiate as toughly as Henry Kissinger, be as great a communicator as Ronald Reagan, listen as well as Dear Abby, have the personality of Oprah Winfrey, and be a clutch performer like Tiger Woods! If you find someone like that, please let me know!

FSBO!

No discussion about buying a home would be complete without having a look at the portion of the market whereby owners try to sell their home themselves. (That topic, from a seller's perspective, is more fully explored in Chapter 3.)

When house hunting, you may come across a private listing, an FSBO. This is quite common. In fact, a recent study showed that agents are involved in about 84% of all resale transactions — meaning about 16% are done privately.[12]

In approaching an FSBO, it's important to first understand the economics. The sellers are trying to get more money by selling the house themselves. The buyers, of course, know this and want to share in the savings. They do this by offering less. That, of course, often undercuts the point of an independent listing from the seller's perspective, and yet is an everyday reality. If the seller will not share in the savings, then you may wind up paying more for the house than you need to. For example, suppose you want to buy a house with a fair market value of $200,000. The house is an FSBO. At 5% commission, the seller is trying to save $10,000. You know this and offer $190,000. The seller responds at $200,000, saying that this is fair value. If you buy the house, you are paying full price but receiving none of the benefits of the buyer's agent. Those benefits can be very valuable.

For example, how do you know what the house is worth? Do you know what the others in the area have sold for, including ones that have recently sold but not closed yet? If it's a condominium and you have a pet, do you know if pets are even allowed? Are the parking spots for the condominium separately deeded or exclusive use? Should you make the offer for a condominium conditional on finding out the state of health of the condominium corporation? Is there something about to happen in the area that the seller does not want you to know? Are you going to rely on what the seller says? When a seller sells without a realtor, they do not have the same disclosure obligations that they would otherwise have. That can be frightening; it means things can be wrong with the house that you might not hear about.

Buying an FSBO without your agent involves a level of risk; assuming that level of risk may not be a reasonable thing to do. Most sellers will work with your buyer's agent and come to terms with them. After all, the seller does want to sell the house, and the simple truth is that most people shop with a realtor. Not having a realtor involved may be a false economy. In other words, there may not be much of a savings, and what looks like a savings may, in reality, be no savings at all, because the advice you might have received may have translated into a better overall deal.

Negotiating

Negotiating is an art, not a science. Buying a house is a bit different than buying a can of beans — the lowest price does not always mean the best overall deal. Rather, the best deal is the result of the price and the terms and whether your emotions about the house are satisfied.

It's probably a mistake to look at the home-buying process as one that only involves money. There is much more to it than that. Think in terms of the difference between a house and a home. A house is a building — and can be purchased devoid of emotion. A home is where you go to unwind, live, raise your family, and feel safe. A home purchase, by necessity, involves an element of emotion and that's what makes negotiating for one so tricky. The key to success in a real estate negotiation is to arrive at a solid balance between the forces of logic and emotion. Too much of either may lead to a bad deal.

Some hard and fast tactics will improve your chances of getting a good deal. There are two basic things to keep in mind when buying real estate. Firstly, you must learn as much as possible about the seller's motivations and financial situation. Secondly, you must learn as much as possible about the property — such as comparable sales — while revealing nothing or next to nothing about your situation.

The following are words to the wise — negotiating tips to help you buy smart!

Figure Out What the House Is Really Worth

Before even thinking of writing up an offer, there are a few necessary steps to consider. The first of these is to get a sense of what the house you are interested in is really worth. That information will guide your path. The most obvious way to arrive at that magical figure is to ask your realtor to do a market analysis. The realtor should be able to tell you with some degree of accuracy what the house is worth by comparing recent sales of houses similar to the one you are considering in the same area. I really do trust the realtors I have worked with, and yet it is still always a good idea for buyers to verify for themselves the accuracy of what the realtor is telling them. One way to do that is to do some legwork on your own — go on the Internet and see what's available in your area yourself so as to form a conclusion as to what the appropriate asking price should be for the house you are interested in. The best sites to go to are listed in Appendix 1 (under "Realtors"). Watch that you are really looking at houses that are comparable to the one you seek. Show the search results to your realtor to verify whether the conclusions you have drawn from your own research are correct. As I've mentioned earlier in the chapter, it's important to verify that you are comparing apples to apples and not apples to oranges.

Yet another option is to seek an independent appraisal. While that will cost a bit of money (at least $150), you will find out the value of the house from a source who has no vested interest in your next steps. They may even tell you what the trend in price has been (if it's downward, you should keep that in mind). Lastly, consider market conditions in making the opening offer. For example, in a hot seller's market, there really is not much point in making an opening "lowball" listing on a desirable property. Assuming you have a good idea what the fair value is for the house in question, it's time for the next step.

Ask a Lot of Questions

Sellers are often instructed to stay out of sight when potential buyers are touring their house, perhaps only meeting a buyer at the end of the whole process. If you do manage to talk to a seller, it's a good idea to ask a lot of questions to learn as much as you can about the property and the seller's true motivation. Sometimes the terms of the agreement can be more important than the price, depending on the seller. You can glean that information if you ask a lot of questions.

For example, everyone should always ask why the seller is selling. This can be valuable information. If the seller has a mortgage that is almost the same as the home value and is in arrears and the bank is about to scoop the house, you want to know (actually, it's always a good idea to do a title search just to see how the mortgage amount relates to the asking price). It's not that you want to take advantage of the hapless homeowner, but that information may help you to better structure your offer. If the seller cannot really afford one more payment, then you want to be sure to make it a quick closing. If you use this valuable information well, both you and the seller should benefit.

You should also try to find out how much the seller paid for the house. This is public record, and available by title search. What the seller paid for the house might not tell you exactly what the market value is, but it does give a clue as to how much room the seller might have, as the original selling point is often a psychological barrier for the seller who likely wants to net at least that amount. In other words, if the seller bought the house 30 years ago, they did not pay anything near what it's worth today. If the terms are right, the seller may part with it for a bit less than it's worth just so as to be done with the whole exercise — since there is such a large profit anyway. The reverse is also true: if the house was recently purchased, then the seller may not be inclined to part with it for less than the original purchase price, regardless of what it's really worth. It's also not a bad idea to ask, in light of what was paid for the house, how the seller arrived at the asking price. The seller will probably give you a market analysis, which you can use to compare with your own research.

The seller should have prepared a disclosure form, outlining known defects. It's always prudent to ask for one of these. While you are on this topic, be sure to ask what defects or problems existed in the past that have already been corrected. If something major was repaired, then you can flag that for the inspection.

Also ask the seller about neighbourhood problems. Noisy neighbours can be a problem and it's a good idea to look into this issue. For crime statistics, ask at your local police station.

Lastly, my favourite question is to ask what the seller thinks the best and worst things are about his or her house. This is a great question (so long as they answer both parts), precisely because it's so open-ended — you never know what they are going to say! If you are able to ask only one question, then this should be the one you ask.

Know When Not To Speak

Once you are ready to sign an offer (having asked all the right questions and having considered the state of the market), the next obvious question is what price to insert. There is no general answer to that question; it depends on your unique situation. One thing that is for certain is that you should not tell your realtor (unless they are your buyer's agent) what your true top line price is. As we saw earlier, if the realtor is the listing agent, then that information can be used against you. Another time it's better not to speak occurs when you see a house and think it is perfect. If you fall in love with a house, and the seller or their agent are around, conveying your enthusiasm will likely only result in the seller being less than anxious to lower the price below the listing price. If you must say anything, try to convey the impression that you could care less whether you buy that house or another one.

Try for a Face-To-Face Meeting with the Seller

Meeting the seller face-to-face provides a great opportunity to ask questions. In addition to the questions outlined above, you should discuss price with the seller and casually ask the seller what their bottom-line price is for the property. In other words, ask whether the price they are asking for the property is the "best" they can do. The key to this type of question is what you do after you ask the question. If you are smart, you will stay silent and let the seller reveal as much as possible. Silence can be golden! The seller may drop the price — perhaps to a number lower than you might otherwise have expected — and you haven't even signed an offer!

Use a Maven

"The Maven" is slang for a supposed "expert" whom you can use as an excuse, "to turn to for guidance." The correct way to use this tactic is to do the best you can in your negotiation, then bring in the "expert" to approve it. The "expert" can be your parents (who may lend you the money) or your spouse (who needs to agree) or perhaps even a trusted adviser. The "expert" always disapproves the best deal and you then get to go back to the drawing board — except you are starting from a much better position, having already beaten down the seller with the first round of negotiating.

Beware the Low-ball Listing

Sometimes (and I think this is a very sleazy practice), a listing will be priced below its true market price. The goal of this trick is to create a feeding frenzy over the house. The rationale is that with buyers bidding against each other for the house, prices are bound to rise — perhaps even higher than the true price. And they very often do.

Depending on the market, this may happen without planning. The question is how you handle this sort of situation. The answer, fortunately, is quite simple: walk away. The only thing that will happen if you stay in the fray is that you might "win" — and wind up overpaying for the house. If you must participate in this sort of negotiation, your best bet is to set a top-line price in your own mind and commit to staying below that number.

You Can Negotiate with Builders, Too

Just because builders are asking a certain price doesn't mean they have no room for flexibility. As with resale houses, it helps to understand the seller's wants and needs. In the case of new houses, the builder is the seller. Builders do not like to drop their asking price because if they do that, it impacts upon the appraised value of all the other homes in the subdivision. In other words, builders have a lot to lose if the perception by appraisers is that the houses they sell are worth anything less than the asking price. If that happens, it can negatively impact future sales. Any time a buyer of another house within the subdivision tries to get financing, the lender will have the house appraised. Nothing could be worse than having the bank tell the buyer that the house is not worth what they paid for it! It may also be that the builders' construction financing is a factor of the appraised value of the finished houses. Because of those needs, you may be better off asking for upgrades to be included in the purchase price — that way, you get something extra (could be nicer floors, appliances, etc.) and builders meet their needs, too. The best way to get a deal from builders, then, is to maintain the posted price but have upgrades included free.

Use the Inspection As a Negotiating Tool

Most people think that their house is nicer and in better shape than it really is. A professional home inspection can usually be relied upon to set the record straight. I definitely recommend having a home inspection before committing to a final purchase. Without an inspection, you may be forced to rely on the representations (or misrepresentations) of the seller. While those representations afford you some protection in law, the reality is that accessing our legal system is very expensive; you are always far better off avoiding the whole mess by having a qualified inspector go over the house with a fine-tooth comb and tell you what the true status is of the house's condition.

Misrepresentations can be innocent. It could be that an elderly widow honestly believed that the roof was new when she said that to the buyer (who then decided not to bother with an inspection) and had no idea that her late husband only reshingled half the roof. In that situation, the buyer was out of luck — and the seller was not responsible for all the money the buyer had to spend on the new roof. The moral of the story: get an inspection!

Most people (77%) obtain an inspection before buying their home.[13] Moreover, 97% of those who obtained an inspection felt that the inspection was "good value" for the price they paid.[14] Those are astonishing numbers.

I suggest negotiating the best deal you can, but insist upon a professional home inspection as a precondition to firming up the deal. Inspectors may indicate approximate dollar values for the repairs they find necessary and should prioritize the deficiencies. They should indicate which repairs should be done immediately and which can wait a year or two.

It's then a good idea to meet with the seller, show them the detailed inspection (and my experience is that inspectors just about always find something wrong), and use the inspection report as a pretext to reopen negotiations. You can either ask for a price reduction, or require the seller to complete some of the work the inspector has recommended. Either way you get another kick at the can. However, the outcome of this strategy depends on the state of the market and the motivations of the seller. In a buyer's market, assuming you are reasonable and not obnoxious about it, this strategy may make a big difference to your overall deal. In a seller's market, it may backfire, unless the seller is strongly motivated to be rid of the house. Tread carefully!

Sometimes, pressure is brought to bear on the buyer to avoid an inspection. This can happen for any number of reasons, but most often the decision to forego an inspection is the result of pressure from the seller, realtor, or the mere presence of a competing buyer. The choice to forego the inspection is individual, but you should know that it could be very expensive to repair defects that may not be visibly apparent, especially to the untrained eye. According to a recent study by Housemaster (a home inspection company), the most common defects found in resale homes are as follows:

- roofing system;

- electrical system;

- plumbing system;

- central heating and cooling;

- insulation;

- structure;

- water seepage.[15]

Even for those buying newly built houses from a builder, it is worth considering an inspection by a professional inspector prior to closing. Some builders will not allow a professional inspector in before the deal closes. The reality, though, is that many buyers assume that because the house is new, that it is exempt from human error. That can be a costly mistake. Especially considering the size of the investment in a house as compared to other investments, making assumptions as to the quality of the builders' work can prove to be a financially devastating error. For example, some defects may only become apparent years after the deal closes, such as when you try to sell and your prospective buyers commission an inspection. The inspector might look and find defects that were not readily apparent, such as in the attic, below the floor, in the chimney, or with the electrical service panel. Defects may be revealed that would have been covered by the original warranty, which may have long since expired. Even if you are buying from a builder, try to have an inspection before closing. It just might be the best money you ever spend.

Things To Keep in Mind

There is a lot to know about when buying a house beyond the mechanics of the process. Timing, how you negotiate, the type of house you buy, and who you hire to help you can all play a significant role in the financial result of your decision.

- Before you even start hunting, find out the type of market the city you want to buy in is experiencing. (Remember that the market in the neighbourhood for the type of home you seek may be different than the market for the city in general.)

- Tap the realtor for information about the type of market and comparables.

- Bear in mind that good deals can be had in any season — the best deals are found when there is an imbalance in supply and demand in the neighbourhood you want for the type of home you seek.

- Remember that any analysis of house values and the factors that influence them involves a certain amount of guesswork. It's important to be an educated consumer — to understand what factors in the past have affected values and what factors in the present are worth considering in evaluating the options.

- Consider buying a "fixer upper" or a house that needs a lot of work; it may be that after renovating, the house's finished value will be greater than the purchase price plus renovations, making it a good investment.

- Understand how to best deal with realtors, including retaining a buyer's agent, signing a buyer agency agreement, and making sure your buyer's agent knows exactly what you want.

- Beware buying an FSBO without an agent, as there may be all kinds of hidden problems.

- Learn how to negotiate from a position of strength, which includes figuring out what the house is really worth, asking a lot of questions, knowing when not to speak, using a maven, and insisting on a home inspection.

In the end, regardless of which factors you choose to place an emphasis on, you have to live in your new home — meaning that you should never underestimate the importance of lifestyle factors and your own personal satisfaction.

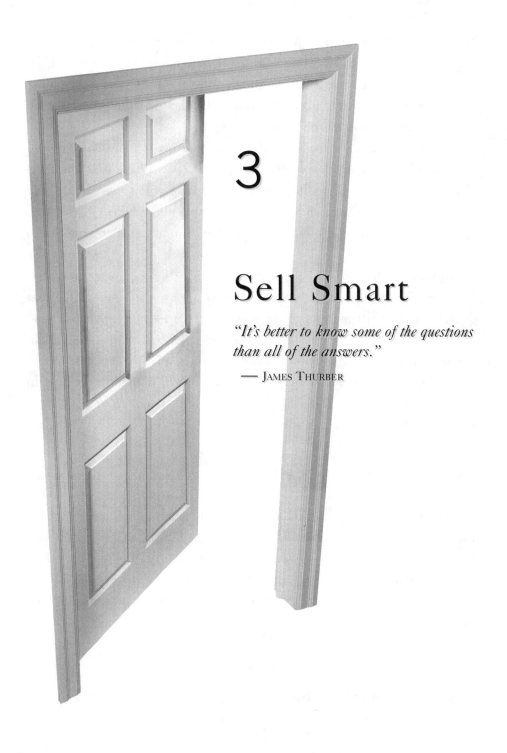

3

Sell Smart

"It's better to know some of the questions
than all of the answers."

— JAMES THURBER

You have your home. You may have gotten it just after being married and may even have had a couple of kids while living there. The walls have pencil markings charting your children's growth spurts, and every room holds special memories of wonderful times. But the rooms are small and the kitchen outdated — it's time to move.

This chapter deals with the harsh reality of money … and how you can get as much of it as possible when selling your house. I have used the word "harsh" deliberately. In selling, emotion and attachment must go out the window. That holds true whether you have lived in the house for 10 years or 10 months. Although it is natural to have an emotional attachment to somewhere you have lived, especially if the place symbolizes major life milestones, you have to find some way to ignore or suppress your emotions. It can be the hardest part of selling. This chapter covers everything from choosing the right time to sell, deciding whether to buy or sell first, and determining an asking price to working with agents and avoiding certain mistakes. It will help you to understand that the moment you decide to sell, your home becomes a *house*, a property to be sold, like a commodity. In selling, it's time to start thinking in dispassionate business terms of how to maximize the return on your investment.

The Best Times To Sell

Timing in life can be everything. Some people seem to have the ability to time a sale just right, almost as if there was some magic to it all. The truth is, there is no magic to timing when it comes to selling a house — just a bit of forethought, common sense, and patience. Applying these principles can make all the difference to the bottom line when it comes to selling your house.

Sell When There Is a Buyer

As we saw in the previous chapter, spring is commonly thought to be the best time to sell. And, in fact, spring is usually the time when many people sell. In the absence of some urgency, many people wait until April or May to list their homes, with closings taking place between May and August. The supply of houses for sale typically starts to shrink in November and does not really get going again until the following spring. A recent study revealed that, 30.2% of home-buying activity takes place in the summer, 25.9% in the spring, 24.8% in the fall, and 19% in the winter.[1] If you follow the herd in listing when everyone else is and selling when everyone else is, you should know that the more homes like yours that buyers have to choose from, the more competition you have and the more selective buyers can be. As a trend, that does not bode well for maximizing the price you get.

"Selling smart" means that you first figure out with your realtor what the supply and demand ratio is like in your neighbourhood before listing the property. If the demand is high, and there are few houses available, that's the right time to sell — even if it's snowing outside!

Sell When There Is a Sense of Urgency

A sense of urgency comes about when buyers feel that something is about to happen, or is in the early stages of happening, that will make houses more expensive or less attainable. It is not to be confused with a false sense of urgency — a common sales trick. A sense of urgency can happen, for example, when people see house prices rising. This can be due to any number of factors, and may be as simple as a particular neighbourhood becoming popular, with prices rising as a result. Or it may well be that the economy is in a growth mode and demand for houses suddenly increases due to heightened consumer confidence, causing a price increase. Those are obviously great times to sell your house. Many people will want to get in on the action before prices rise too much and the house becomes unaffordable for them. Similarly, if interest rates are rising, many buyers will want to take advantage of the prevailing rates and beat any future price increases. On the other hand, a false sense of urgency typically does not relate to prevailing economic conditions, but rather to rhetoric such as a realtor telling you something so as to inspire anxiety ("You had better sell now before the neighbours put their house on the market," and so on).

If the economic climate is favourable to the seller — and prices and/or interest rates are rising — you may be well advised to sell the house before the market shifts in another direction.

Sometimes it makes sense to sell in the right economic climate, to get the most money for your house, but you might not be quite ready to move. It may be that interest rates are rising and the buyers want to close before rates go up any more but really don't need to be in the house for a while. If that happens, consider trying to close the sale but renting the house back for a short time from the buyers. That way you get the higher price and the buyers get to take advantage of the lower interest rate. But the buyer does take on a risk by having you as tenant. The buyer has to trust that you will, in fact, be a good tenant and also leave when the agreed-upon term expires (some people have been known to break the agreement if the house they have purchased does not close for whatever reason and they need somewhere to stay until they find a replacement). At the minimum, if you do sell before you're ready, you can set a long closing date (beware the low deposit!) to give you sufficient time to find a new house.

Sell Before You Really Have To

Another study[2] found that 24% of sellers had to sell their homes quickly because they had already bought another house. A further 11% were in a rush to sell because they had already moved out or were in the process of moving out.

If you are in a rush to sell, that element of desperation is almost certain to become apparent to a potential buyer. There is no better way to harm your maximum return on investment than to have to sell in a rush or to have any element of desperation added to the transaction. Buyers have an uncanny way of sniffing out that sort of problem and it will work to your detriment. You are far better off having time on your side. If you have time, you will not feel as pressured to grab the first deal that comes by, but rather will wait until a fair offer is presented.

At the other end of the spectrum, waiting too long can also cost you. Seniors can be especially bad at waiting too long to sell their house. Their reticence to leave is totally understandable, as they may have spent a large part of their lives in the home they are being asked to sell, but they may end up losing or not getting as much money as they could have. What often happens is that seniors are advised to trade down into a smaller, lower maintenance house, but because they might have waited so long to sell, they have neglected the maintenance of the house. A house that hasn't been maintained will certainly have less value. As a general rule, you should always keep your house in the best condition possible.

Buy or Sell First?

The goals in the delicate balancing act of deciding whether to buy or sell first are to avoid wasting money carrying two residences at once and to sell in such a way that you get as much return as possible.

Generally, the rule of thumb is that it is better to sell first in a buyer's market and buy first in a seller's market. In a buyer's market, prices are falling, so it makes sense to get the house sold first, before prices fall any further. In a buyer's market, selling can be difficult; you want some certainty that you don't have to worry (unless the deal does not close) about the expense of carrying two houses at once. A buyer's market may be the right time to trade up to a more expensive house because while you may net less from your existing house, you will also certainly pay less for the more expensive home. It's the spread between the two that you need to look at, and that spread may be lower in a buyer's market than a seller's market.

The reverse logic holds true for what to do in a seller's market. In that market, buying can be difficult, so it makes sense to buy first. Otherwise, you may find yourself in the awkward predicament of having sold the house and not having a replacement house to go to (can you say mother–in–law?). In a seller's market, there is an advantage for you as a seller but a disadvantage for you as a buyer.

Advantages of Selling First

Unfortunately, the entire issue of whether to buy or sell first is not that clear-cut. The general rules do not apply to all situations, and it's better to pay attention to particular situations rather than be guided solely by general guidelines. Consider the following factors.

No Double Mortgage

Sometimes, it makes sense to sell first for no other reason than to avoid the burden of carrying two houses. If you have bought first and are then unable to sell your existing house, you will still be obligated to the deal you have committed to. You will then have two main options: you can carry the mortgage on both houses out of your own cash flow (if you can afford to), or you can apply to a lender for interim financing. Interim financing means that a lender lends you the money to close the first deal. This can be a good, short-term solution. The lender, in assessing the loan, will look at your creditworthiness, how good the prospects are of your selling your existing home, and what security they can get out of the equity in your house. While this is often a good option in a pinch, be forewarned that it can be very expensive, as you will essentially be carrying three mortgages on two homes (your own first mortgage, the new house first mortgage, and a second mortgage on your existing house — which the lender will likely require as additional security). Moreover, approvals can be difficult to obtain.

If you have already sold the first house but the closing of your sale is after the closing on the purchase, and as a result you only need the money for a short time, it's often much easier to obtain a basic loan for that specific period of time. This type of loan is called bridge financing.

Note: If you do not have the ability to close the deal you have committed to because you cannot sell your existing home, you can reasonably expect to be responsible for the seller's losses. The seller, in that situation, usually will remarket the property. If the seller is only able to sell it for less (assuming the house is sold at fair market value), you will be responsible for the difference between what you were supposed to pay and what the seller actually received, plus any carrying costs in the interim. Another remedy is for the seller to apply to the courts for an order forcing the buyer to fulfill their contractual obligations. This remedy is not commonly used, as it is more sensible to remarket the property and then attempt to recover whatever financial loss there may be. Not closing can be a very expensive proposition! Not only is there the cost of making the seller whole (putting the seller in the position they would have been in financially had you fulfilled the contract), but entering the world of litigation (lawyers can be devastating to anyone's pocketbook). My advice — avoid lawsuits like the plague. For these reasons alone, many sellers prefer to breathe easy and sell first.

No "Rush" Sale

If you sell first, you avoid the problem of the sense of urgency in selling. Remember: most buyers or their agents will sniff your sense of desperation; it makes good sense not to even have to consider that as a possibility. One of the worst things that can happen to your pocketbook is to fall in love with another house and then have to hurry your existing house onto the market so that you can sell it and use the proceeds to buy the dream home. You may not get the full value out of the house. I know some realtors who will suggest that you not even look at other houses before you have sold for this reason. I don't agree with that rationale, but often realtors do all the work for the new house, only to have it fall apart if you can't close because you haven't sold your old house. Frankly, it's a good idea, even before you sell, to have a look at the market if for no other reason than to see whether you can afford the new house. And it's a good way to see whether your expectations are reasonable. For example, if you are selling so as to buy a bigger house and think that the affordable difference in price between the house you have and the house you want is around $100,000, then you should verify that the difference is what you think it is.

Ability To Negotiate from a Position of Strength

Another nice thing about selling first is that it allows you to be very aggressive in negotiating your purchase. Since you more or less have the money from the sale to spend, you are in a much stronger bargaining position than other potential buyers, who may be worried about selling their home and may load the offer up with conditions designed to protect them from the prospect of carrying two homes. Negotiating from a position of strength is ideal. Having sold your house, you can make an all cash offer and know with some certainty when you will be able to close.

Disadvantages of Selling First

While there are many reasons why it's sensible to sell first, there are also some factors to consider that are not all that positive.

Settling for Another House

Sometimes, having sold first, you find yourself with a looming closing date and no house to buy that you really like. When that happens, you are under some pressure to find something fast and may as a result settle for a house that's not exactly what you really wanted, just because you want to have somewhere to move into after the sale closes. Not only are you prone to getting something you may not really want, but the "pressure" of having to be in somewhere by a looming deadline may inspire you to pay more than you might otherwise have, just to have a place to live.

Interim Housing

Another potential downside is that if you sell and have been unable to find another house, you may have to enter the world of interim housing. That can involve significant expense in that you will have to have furniture packed and unpacked and moved and perhaps have some put into storage. It may also be tricky to find a short-term rental if you have pets, as many landlords are not "pet-friendly." Lastly, there may be a significant price to pay in your stress level as you are either uprooting the family or, sometimes worse, living with relatives. It's worth thinking twice about the total impact of having to acquire an interim residence.

Showing the House

You've evaluated the market and made some tough choices about when to sell and whether to buy or sell first, and the time has come to move forward. There are things you can do to increase the saleability and the amount of money you get for your house. Surprisingly, the things to do are simple and the financial rewards can be great.

Tidy Up and Depersonalize

Making your house look tidy and uncluttered is one of the very first things you should do when selling a house. You want prospective buyers to be able to come in and visualize their things in your house. Put yourself in the shoes of the home shopper. You go into a house. The inside is full of stuff — family pictures, awards, gifts, knick-knacks, and more. What do you look at first? Most likely, you will, out of curiosity, look at all the little things lying around, rather than focusing on the interior layout of the house and imagining how your things would fit into the rooms. At the end of the day, when people have looked at a bunch of houses, it's hard for them to remember one from another. If you are selling your home, you should tidy up all those little things that tend to pile up at the front door, on kitchen counters, etc., and take down all those family photos on shelves and corner tables. In fact, what you're doing is depersonalizing your home by removing items of a unique or personal nature. It's also good to clear out excess furniture. Your goal is to make it easy for prospective buyers to imagine themselves in your house. You want to focus them on purchasing. The fewer distractions around, the better.

Fix Obvious Things

You certainly don't need to undertake major renovations, but it's imperative that minor repairs be done before selling. Make sure that all the appliances work, that all the light bulbs are intact, and that all paint touch-ups have been done, among other things.

Clean and Then Clean Again!

Few things are worse for shoppers than walking into a house that is not clean. How do you think shoppers will feel if they run into cobwebs while walking through the house? Clean everything — the windows, rugs, floors, bathtubs, and more. It may add to the shopper's "first impression." Remember: you never get a second chance to make a first impression.

Consider a Home Inspection

Most buyers will have the home inspected before they finalize a contract. Given this knowledge, it makes good sense to find out what the inspector will say before you actually list the house. A home inspection gives you a chance to fix whatever is wrong before the house goes onto the market. Some sellers like to supply a copy of the inspection to prospective buyers. That can be a nice touch; it shows that you have nothing to hide and may allow a deal to proceed without the slowdown of an inspection. I think a pre-inspection is money well spent.

Consider a Decorator

If your house is not well furnished, it can make sense to hire a decorating service that rents furniture. That way, the house will look great for the showings. A house that "shows well" might sell before one that does not. This is a relatively new trend that, in my mind, makes a lot of sense.

Turn on the Air Conditioning and Do the Lawn

If you are showing your house during the summer, there are a few things you can do to make the house more saleable. For starters, make sure the air conditioning is on when any potential buyers tour the house. The last thing you want is for a prospective buyer to be turned off because they are uncomfortable in a house that is too hot. The extra cost of keeping the house cool for them is money well spent. It's also a good idea to keep the lawn well-watered — nothing is more appealing than a green, rich-looking lawn. Dry or brown grass and shrubbery can be a big turnoff for prospective buyers.

Bake Bread

Most people like the aroma of fresh-baked bread. It makes the house feel more "homey." In fact, the 2001 National Home Attitude Poll[3] indicated that for more than one-third of Canadians, the smell of fresh-baked bread helped sell them on a home.

The Asking Price

Setting the asking price is a delicate matter. There are lots of old wives' tales floating around, just ready to misguide sellers. For example, some people are of the view that houses should be priced higher than they are worth so as to allow room to manoeuvre and negotiate. The problem in overpricing the house is that the only thing of value you may be doing is helping to sell the house down the street that is more fairly priced! Most of the activity on the house (i.e., number of showings and offers) will take place when it first becomes available. That's when those in the market and realtors take their first look and gain their first impression. If you overprice the house, you lose the impact of a good first impression because those who are really interested may not be able to afford to take a shot at your house. Even if you subsequently lower the price, the interest level of prospective buyers may have already diminished. Not pricing the house fairly means it is destined to stay on the market longer, which is usually a bad situation. One of the first things shoppers invariably ask is, "How long has the house been on the market?" If it has been on the market for "a while" (it's anybody's guess as to what that means), then many shoppers draw the adverse conclusion that there is something wrong with the house. You are less likely to maximize the selling price if shoppers think something is wrong with the house. Best bet? Don't overprice the house. Conversely, as we saw in the previous chapter, some realtors believe that the best thing to do is to deliberately underprice the house. The thinking is that if the house is priced below fair market value then buyers will rush into a feeding frenzy and bid against one another until they bid the price up beyond fair market value. This is not only a very sleazy manoeuvre, but it could also backfire. Buyers, especially those represented by a buyer's agent, may recognize the scheme for the reprehensible practice that it is, and choose not to bother with your house. Worse yet, other realtors may shun your home, meaning it may sit on the market for the dreaded "a while" — the kiss of death to getting a great return on the house sale.

There is no such thing as an exact price for your house. Any house is only worth what someone is willing to pay for it. The trick is to find an asking price that is fair value. And the best way to find what that is is to ask a good local realtor to provide you with what realtors call "comps" (comparative market valuations). They will look at recent sales of similar properties in the same neighbourhood. Real estate trades or sales are reported into a database, and a skilled realtor will know exactly and quickly how to arrive at the calculation.

Many realtors will provide you with a comparative market analysis for free — with the hope that you will list with them. It's probably a good idea to interview a few realtors before selecting one anyway, and one thing you can ask them all for is the same market analysis to see if they differ from one another in some way. Beware of the realtors who suggest a price much higher than the average that you receive — they may be trying to put stars in your eyes by lulling you into a false sense of what the house is really worth. Similarly, it's probably a good idea to question the realtor with the lowest suggested market value. Another option is to hire a professional appraiser to give you an opinion on the value of the house. The nice thing about doing that is that the appraiser, unlike any of the realtors, has no vested interest in what you do. The appraiser is not trying to sell you anything beyond the appraisal service. While it may cost $150 for a drive-by appraisal, it's a great way to find out what the true market price is for your house.

Yet another option is to go to the Internet or the classified ads to see what the asking prices are for houses like yours. While there is a big difference between the asking price and the actual value, the reality is that asking prices are generally not more than 10% above the actual value; they can be relied on for a sense of what is going on in the market for your type of house. Remember that you need to try to compare apples to apples and in doing that consider the impact of location. Other houses may be similar to yours physically, but may have a great view (adding to value) or be in a bad or high traffic area (lowering value).

If you want to sell your house quickly and get the most money for it, price the house fairly based on its location, features, and state of the market. You want to get a pool of buyers interested as quickly as possible in the house. If it is priced fairly, that is more likely to happen because those looking (and their agents) will know the house is priced fairly, hence it is likely to "go" quickly — so the agents rush to bring their clients to see it. That, in turn, creates a sense of urgency that is the sellers' utopia. If there is a sense of urgency, then shoppers may bid against one another for the house. When that happens, the selling price inevitably goes up!

Realtors

In selling, the amount of money that finds its way into your jeans is really the bottom line. The greatest impact on what that bottom-line number will be has to do with the role of the realtor in the transaction. Just as there are for buyers, there are a couple of choices for sellers as to whether they use a realtor or sell privately. And the key consideration is money. Realtor commissions average about 5% of the sale price. (Bear in mind that 5% is not what your realtor actually gets — the total is subject to splits and their expenses.) No matter how you slice it, 5 to 6% off the top of anything is a lot of money, and some consumers question the worth of this commission. In other words, some consumers do not feel that the 5 to 6% they spend on realtors is a good deal.

Do realtors really add value consistent with the cost of their services? The answer lies in understanding what value realtors lend to the transaction. Answering this question requires an explanation of the realtors' role in the process. In the ideal world, the cost of the realtor pales in significance to the value they add.

Here is what a full-service or "good value" realtor should do for you.

Pre-Sale Advice

The "good value" realtor will visit your house, look around, and advise you on what you need to do to get the house ready for sale so as to get the highest possible sale price. This advice ranges from cleaning up clutter to what minor repairs need to be done to your house in your market. In other words, rather than provide general advice, you should receive advice specific to your house. The "good value" realtor will tell you that if you want to get the most money for the house, you need to realize that the way you live in the house is not necessarily the same thing as the way you sell the house. Being open-minded about changing things within the house will help you maximize the sale price. You can get more money for the house by heeding the realtor's advice on what to do to get the house ready for sale.

Listing Price

You don't want to guess on what price to ask for your house, nor do you want to underprice or overprice. A realtor will help you decide what the right list price is for your home, a decision that is based on their experience in the area as well as on a market analysis. You can get more money for your house by listing it at the right price — and the realtor can help you determine what that price should be.

MLS and a Marketing Plan

There really is nothing quite like the Multiple Listing Service (MLS). You want to let as many people as possible know about your house being up for sale. A more efficient system to do that simply does not exist. Basically, the system works by posting your listing onto a computer program that all realtors who are properly licensed have access to. The very first thing most realtors do when searching for houses is to check the MLS system to see what is available. The system cannot be accessed directly by the public, although public Web sites, such as Homestore.ca, mls.ca, and Homeadvisor.ca, contain some of the same fields of information in an increasingly fast time frame.

Think in terms of supply and demand. Prices rise in large part because of supply and demand. Your house being for sale is part of the supply. You want to increase demand and the best way to do this is by exposing your house in every way possible: people cannot buy something they do not know about. But most buyers will use a realtor and all realtors use the MLS system. Some realtors will try to persuade you to list your house on an "exclusive" basis with his or her company only. Beware. You are always better off having the house on the MLS system — that way, all realtors in town (and those abroad who are looking) will be able to find out about it. The last thing you want is to entertain an offer from a client brought in on an exclusive listing and then find out afterwards that a client of another agency would have paid more. The most important part of any realtor's marketing plan is to have the house on this system. The realtor should devise a total plan, including neighbourhood flyers, newspaper, and Internet ads aimed both at potential buyers and at other realtors.

Lawn Sign and Screening

The realtor will place a "For Sale" sign on the lawn of your house. True, anyone can do that, but the realtor likely has a 24/7 paging system — meaning that they can return all calls at any time from prospective buyers or other realtors who drive by and see the sign and have questions. You may not be able to do that during work hours and may not appreciate or have the skill to weed out real prospects from dreamers when you receive calls. Frankly, your time is money. Having someone be available at all times to answer questions about your house and to identify real prospects is worth paying for.

Marketing Brochures

There is a true art to creating a good marketing brochure. A realtor's brochure should describe what's best about your house and should be given out to those who inquire about the house, or at showings, and/or may even be left in a box outside the house for prospects to pick up and review on their own. Some people are never sold on anything right away but rather need time to consider and plan. For this type of buyer especially, a good, detailed brochure is ideal. If designed well, it can make a difference in how interested a given prospect will be. Realtors design these pieces as part of their everyday business. You can get more money for your house by covering all bases, including having a great brochure designed by a realtor.

Caravan Tours

When obtaining a new listing, a realtor should arrange for your house to be featured on what they call a "caravan." Typically, real estate offices have weekly meetings. When the meeting ends, a group of the realtors will drive around the neighbourhood together, inspecting each and every new listing. This allows the other agents within the office to gain firsthand a sense of what your house is all about. It's more effective than looking at a picture alone or gazing at a computer screen. Sometimes, after the caravan, other realtors in the office contact their prospects and can answer questions effectively since they have been inside the house. Just as you want to expose your house to as many buyers as possible, you also want to expose it to as many realtors as possible in order to have the best chance of selling for the most money.

Advice on Market Conditions

A good realtor will be able to let you know what is going on in your local market on an ongoing basis. Issues may arise that you need to be aware of because they impact your sale. If the house does not sell in the first two weeks after appearing on the market, you need to know why, what has sold, and why competitors have sold when you have not been able to. Keeping tabs on the competition is a regular part of the realtor's world. Remember, there are three general reasons why a house has not sold: location, price, and condition. You can't do much about the location, but the realtor can advise you on issues relating to price and condition. Knowing the inside scoop on what has been selling and what conditions impact your sale can help you get more money than operating in a vacuum.

Open Houses

I've included this as something of value a realtor does for you because, once in a while, someone actually sells his or her house as a result of an open house. But keep in mind that most of the time, the open house is more of a benefit to the realtor than the seller. The realtor looks to the open house as a way to meet new clients. Open houses are great ways to pander to the inner desires of nosy neighbours — many of whom view an open house as a great way to see how their neighbours (you) live. When else will they have a chance to check out your furniture? An open house is a good way to keep your house in the public eye, but don't be fooled: houses rarely sell as a result of an open house.

Negotiations and Showings

One of the worst things any negotiator can do is to be emotionally involved in the outcome of the sale. Typically, realtors are not constrained by this impediment. Realtors receive training in negotiating skills and, because it's not their house, they can be more objective than some sellers. Selling your house is your realtor's area of expertise. Sellers, on the other hand, have other things going on in their lives and may not have the time or the stomach to show people through their prized possession. That sort of thing is best left to an expert.

Final Note

In selecting the right realtor be sure to consider asking tough questions, such as:

- Why should I hire you?

- How long have you been in the business?

- How many listings do you have?

- What references can you provide?

- Are you full-time or part-time?

Remember, this is a business issue. Do not hire a realtor because you like them or they appear to be "nice." And think twice about part-time realtors. If you are considering hiring someone who works part-time, ask yourself whether it really is prudent to entrust the sale of your most valuable asset to someone who is doing something else between 9 and 5 every day. You are looking for a shark who will ruthlessly hunt down prospects and work each deal so as to squeeze as much money out of the transaction on your behalf.

What About Just Selling the House Yourself?

At first blush, selling the house yourself may seem attractive. After all, who wouldn't want to be able to keep the entire sale proceeds and not have to pay 5% or more out of the net? Do you really need to support all those realtors and their fancy cars? If your goal is to get as much money for the house as possible, avoiding an expense may seem sensible.

Balancing this notion are three concepts, namely, that of a false economy, understanding what the savings potential truly is, and the newer option of discount realtors and unbundled and shared services.

False Economy

The National Association of Realtors recently put out a study that showed the median selling price of houses sold by owners on average was $16,000 less than houses sold using a real estate agent.[4] Moreover, the same study asked people who entered the FSBO (For Sale By Owner) world what their experience was like. Half of them vowed they would never do it again. Those people complained about the hassle of holding open houses, arranging appraisals and inspections, dealing with the paperwork and the buyer's financing, and simply having to devote so much time to get the job done right. By trying to sell by yourself, are you being "penny wise and pound foolish"? In other words, while it might look like a cost savings, does it mean that the house may sit on the market longer, that it doesn't get exposed correctly, and that the end sale result is less? The answer to all three questions, in my opinion, is an absolute yes.

When selling alone, generally the exposure your house will get is limited to what people say about your house from seeing the lawn sign and what benefit you gain from a classified ad in the local paper. There are a number of Internet sites you can go to (forsalebyowner.ca, solosale.ca, privatelist.ca, etc.), but none of them dominates. The truth is that the number of people who go to any of the FSBO sites is only a tiny fraction of the number of people who go to the mainstream sites such as mls.ca, homestore.ca, or homeadvisor.ca — all of whom only display ads where the houses are listed with a realtor. Moreover, FSBO deals, by their very nature, preclude exposure to out-of-town buyers, who will not be able to drive by or see the ad in the local paper, or who may not be aware of any of the FSBO sites. The ads in the paper, in any event, can only say so much — not nearly as much as some of the virtual tours available on the mainstream Internet sites. FSBO may sound nice, but it makes more sense to expose your house to as wide a group of potential buyers as possible — and that is accomplished through a realtor and the MLS system.

Also, the FSBO sites on the Internet generally provide tons of advice on everything ranging from how to get the house ready for sale to handling the house inspection, dealing with complex buyer issues, structuring the trans-action, and more. The fact that they do this, in my mind, means that there are a lot of things people really need to know. If there is so much to know, does it make sense not to have a professional guide you?

And when you factor in the reduced exposure, the value of your time in handling the showings, appraisals, inspections, negotiations, the increased legal expense, and the risk of not having benefited from professional advice at all stages of the transaction, the conclusion of false economy becomes clear.

What the Savings Potential Truly Is

Think about it. You are selling your home alone. The buyer may also not be represented. Do you really think the buyer does not recognize these savings? The buyer certainly does and will almost always want some of the savings — and you can bet that will come out in the negotiations. Anyone familiar with FSBO will tell you that it is perfectly ordinary and reasonable for the savings to somehow be reflected in the ultimate purchase price, meaning the seller and the buyer share in the money not being spent. If you think you will save 6% by selling yourself, you are sadly mistaken — I've never heard of it happening. Most buyers have agents anyway. Those agents, usually buyer's agents, will be happy to work with you, but they have to be paid. Whether you pay them or the buyer pays them, either way, it comes out of your pocket — and this will likely be reflected in the price they are able to offer you for the house. The point is that with a FSBO it is not correct to think that you will save the whole 6%. You may save something, but not the whole amount of the commission that a full-service agent would have charged.

Discount Realtors and Unbundled Services

Similarly, just because you use a realtor does not automatically mean that you will spend a full 6% on the commission. Many realtors these days offer a menu of choices: you pay for what you use. This is known as "unbundled services." Another option is to select a discount realtor — one who offers you less service in exchange for a lower commission. Essentially, a discount realtor still offers a "bundle" of services — it's just that there is less in the bundle. Discount realtors are sort of a cross between a FSBO and a full-service realtor. While I clearly do not like FSBO I am less wary of discount brokers.

Some discounters advertise a deal such as a 2% commission. Beware! It's usually not that at all. If your house is going onto the MLS (and it should), remember that while you are free to make whatever up-front deal you want with your realtor for services in selling the property, chances are that the buyer will come with his or her own agent — and that agent is going to want to get paid. The buyer's agent is in a strong bargaining position because he or she has the buyer. Most of the time, you can only play with the half of the commission that the listing agent (your agent) could potentially be entitled to; it's much more difficult to play games with the buyer's agent. In other words, you may pay 2% or less commission, but that's just to your agent. The other agent also wants and deserves to get paid.

When you hire a realtor who offers the option of a lower commission in exchange for fewer services, you are essentially identifying what services typically offered by the full-service realtor that you either do not want or are prepared to take on your own. After all, if you help sell the property, why wouldn't the realtor share his or her fees with you? It is an old truism of business efficiency that tasks should ideally be performed by those suited to performing them. It may well be that you are comfortable doing some of the tasks that the realtors typically perform, such as arranging and attending all showings of the house (how hard is it to say, "this is the kitchen, this is the bathroom, this is the dining room … ?") If the prospect is really interested, then at that time you can call in the realtor to help. It's important to be absolutely clear what tasks you are doing and what the realtor is supposed to do. For example, it may be that you want some of the realtor's expertise, but not all. It may be that you want the house on the MLS and you'd like the realtor's pre-sale advice, listing price advice, and negotiation skills. In that case, you may do some of the advertising and arrange for all showings.

It may be that you will only call the realtor in when you feel you have a "hot" prospect. Remember, the realtor has only their time and expertise to sell. If you use less of it, it makes sense to pay less. Some discount realtors do nothing more than take a listing and post it onto the MLS, but most consumers need more than that. Some less-than-scrupulous discount realtors have been known to do not a thing more than list it onto the MLS, hoping for a quick sale. When that does not happen, and you want more services, the bundle that you have committed to (they make you sign a listing agreement) may not include what you need. If you then turn to another realtor to help you, that new realtor may decline because you have a listing agreement with another broker. As with so many things in life, when it comes to discount or reduced services in selling your house, go into it with both eyes open!

The balance you have to achieve is between having a trusted expert represent you, fight for you, and handle the transaction and potentially saving a few bucks. Be careful. You may not be saving as much as you think.

Expensive Mistakes

Anything worth doing is worth doing properly. In order to do something properly, you have to know both what to do and what not to do. When selling a house, there's really no room for mistakes, as they can end up costing you quite a lot. It's important to review the following so that you don't inadvertently sell yourself short.

Choosing the First Realtor You Meet To List the House

Realtors know that the first realtor you interview has the best chance of being hired. The National Association of Realtors has shown that 63% of sellers only interviewed one realtor before listing their house.[5] If you hire the first realtor who is first able to secure an appointment with you, you may be hiring the one with the best skills at getting appointments with sellers to list as opposed to the one with the best marketing plan and negotiation skills. It's prudent to ask around, obtain references, and interview a few realtors before making a selection.

Choosing the Realtor Who Gave You the Highest Suggested Listing Price for Your House

Many sellers tend to think that their house is worth more than it really is. Some realtors take advantage of that and suggest a listing price that is higher than fair value for the house. They do that in part to pander to the seller's ego, which is generally flattered at the notion that someone else also thinks the house is worth the higher price. In the realtor business, this is called "buying" a listing. This can cost you a lot of money. Egos are best left aside when it comes to pricing houses. As we saw earlier, listing too high can have disastrous consequences for your bank account, especially if the house ends up sitting on the market for a long time. The market value is the market value — it's a matter of fact. The various realtors you interview should all produce market values close to one another. If one is too high, you'll probably be better off not picking that realtor. The most common result of listing too high is that your final sale price will probably be lower than if you listed it at fair value in the first place.

Not Paying Attention To a Proper Marketing Plan

Some realtors' ideas of a marketing plan is placing a sign on the lawn and an ad in the local classifieds (one of the key benefits of the realtors' classified ads is for the realtor to attract other new clients). A good marketing plan should include more than lawn signs and classified ads. It should include targetting buyers outside of the local area — possibly nationally or even internationally. It should also include a personalized "Just Listed" flyer sent out door-to-door in the area and in nearby areas, Internet advertising, a nice brochure showing off the best features of the house, and more. Beware of realtors who do not have a comprehensive plan as to how they intend to sell your house.

Not Getting the House Ready for Sale

Earlier in this chapter we reviewed some of the various things that can be done to get a house ready for sale, such as removing clutter and cleaning.

Some sellers think that just because they may be in a "good'" market, that means they don't really have to do anything to get the house ready for sale. That's dangerous thinking! You may seriously shortchange yourself by failing to get the house ready.

Insisting on Having an Open House

From a seller's perspective, the open house is almost always a waste of time, since it's a lot of work and rarely results in a sale. Many sellers insist on it, in part because they like to see the realtor working. The most likely outcome of an open house is that you will help your realtor get new clients. Unless that is what you want to do, you may be better off directing your energies elsewhere.

Hanging Around During Initial Showings and Open Houses

Very often, sellers hang around during showings or open houses. This can be stressful for everyone and can undermine the potential effectiveness of the showings. Sellers typically are tempted to show off improvements — not realizing that they are probably better off allowing potential buyers to see the house on their own. Realtors worry a lot (justly so) about the seller saying something that will somehow be either misinterpreted by the buyer or which will somehow offend or upset them (the seller could say that there are lots of kids in the neighbourhood and the buyer may have just had a miscarriage) or for that matter, saying something silly, such as making a big deal about unimportant improvements.

Sometimes, if you are home and are hanging around one room (thinking it's best to stay out of the buyers' way), buyers end up overlooking that room or discounting it when they do their assessment of the house. Because of that, the tour of the house may not be truly complete. Buyers may be a bit intimidated by your presence and as a result, not look at the house as thoroughly as they might otherwise have, had you not been there. Generally, realtors don't want you hanging around for showings. Your best bet (assuming your package with the realtor includes the realtor doing the showings) is to listen to the advice the realtor gives you and let them control the initial showings.

The same is not necessarily true for subsequent showings, where there are some good reasons to let the buyer and seller meet so that the negotiation becomes less adversarial.

Talking Too Much

There is an old saying that all sellers should pay attention to: "God gave you two ears and one mouth — use it in that proportion." When it comes to selling your house, the less said by the seller the better. If you must be home during a showing, do yourself a favour and say nothing to the buyer or his or her agent beyond the initial greeting. Ideally, if you must speak, say nothing more than that you are on your way out and that you will be available later to answer any questions. As we saw above, you are better off not getting into a discussion with the buyers. (They might have read the "buyer" chapter of this book and be ready with the right sort of questions — strictly designed to see what they can get out of you.) If you need friendly banter, call a friend!

The realtor should be there for the showing assuming this is part of the "bundle" you've paid for and has an essential function to perform. You are likely paying him or her anyway; why not stay out of the way? For example, you might mention to the buyer that something in the house is "new." Your definition of "new" and theirs may be completely different. After all, you might have been living there for 20 years and something that you put in three years ago would be new to you. The buyer may think that anything not installed that year is not new. The buyer may ask you how many showings you have had of the house. If you have had a lot of showings and say so, the buyer may wonder why no one has bought the house yet — perhaps there is something wrong with it? If you have not had too many showings and say so, the buyer may wonder why no one is looking at the house — perhaps there is something wrong with it? You might say something about how quiet the neighbourhood is, not realizing that the prospective buyer wants to be somewhere socially active where they can make new friends. You might tell the buyer that you have already bought another house, thereby exposing a weakness in that there is some pressing urgency for you to sell the house. You don't need to run the risk of putting your foot in your mouth — just stay away and don't talk to prospective buyers. Let the realtor do the talking for you!

Expecting To Get All the Money Back from Improvements

As we saw in Chapter 2, many people think that if they spend $10,000 on a given improvement, they should get at least that much more for the house. The fact is that some improvements simply do not pay for themselves. The market value of the house should reflect its overall condition, factoring in the improvements you have done. Generally, an improved house is worth more than an unimproved one, but it is an error to isolate one improvement and expect the sale price to allow you to recoup 100% of the cost of that specific improvement.

Not Insisting on Feedback

Your realtor should find out what people think of the house following showings. This information can be crucial in trying to figure out why your house might have been shown many times, but not have received any offers. Be sure you get a detailed report following each showing. But remember: the realtor is not merely an order-taker. If they give you valuable feedback accompanied by a recommendation based on their experience, you are well advised to give careful consideration to what you are being told.

Thinking That Values Must Only Go Up

Values for real estate fluctuate. Sometimes they go down. The real estate market is not drastically different than the stock market, in fact. If you bought a stock three years ago for $100 per share and it is now worth $40 per share, would you expect to sell it for your original cost plus a profit? You can only sell it for what it's worth on the current market. Real estate is no different. For some reason, sellers have trouble with this concept and think that their house is always worth what they paid for it, plus some appreciation. It doesn't work that way. Your house is worth only what someone will pay. Being stubborn about a price and expecting more than fair market value will only result in your house attracting a stigma when it sits unsold on the market.

Hiring a Rude Agent

Some realtors have a reputation in the business as rude, arrogant, or hard to get along with. Other agents may avoid those agents' listings, because they don't want to work with them and so your house may sit on the market longer because it will be exposed to fewer potential buyers than it might otherwise be. You want to avoid hiring an agent like that. Ideally, your realtor should have the respect of others in the community and be enthusiastic and cooperative. For these reasons, it's worth investigating the realtor's reputation by asking around and checking out the references you get.

Accepting a Bad Contingent Sales Offer

Sometimes, you receive an offer that you want to take, but the buyer still needs to sell his or her own house and so makes an offer to you conditional on the sale of his or her existing house. That can work well or can be a waste of your time and create lost opportunity, depending on how you go about it. A conditional offer of this sort is not necessarily a bad thing; it only means that you have to take some precautions. After all, it may be that your house is a hard sell and you want to work with whoever is interested. On the other hand, you may lose some control over the outcome of the dual transaction.

If you do sell conditional on the sale of the buyer's existing house, consider the following.

- Learn about the other property to help figure out if it is priced to sell or not.

- Require the prospective buyer to price their house at a number that your realtor approves of.

- If the buyer does not welcome your realtor approving the listing price, require the buyer to reduce the listing price by a few percent every two weeks for a specified time until the house sells.

- Be sure the time frame conditions are crystal clear and include two times, namely, one for the buyer to enter into an agreement to sell his or her property and another for the closing of the two deals. This allows you some leeway (for example, you might allow the buyer 15 days to find someone to buy his or her house and another 30 days for the deals to close. If the buyer cannot find someone within the 15-day time frame, you have a right to sell to someone else or you can renegotiate another time frame).

- Insert a release or right of first refusal clause. If you have a clause that allows the buyer a set time frame within the earlier condition to firm up based on your having received another offer, you can then continue to market the property. Although this does offer you some measure of protection, the reality is that other realtors sometimes tend not to want to show your house to their prospects because word gets out that your house is subject to another contract.

Things To Keep in Mind

There is a 90/10 unwritten rule when it comes to realtors — that is, 10% of them do 90% of the business.

I imagine that the same can be said for people who sell their houses: 90% of them have not gone about it in such a way as to get the most money possible. You want to be in the top 10%, those who have thought the whole thing through and made wise choices.

- Determine when the best time to sell is, taking into consideration whether there is a buyer or a sense of urgency or an opportunity to sell before you really have to (and thus avoid an element of desperation).

- Decide whether to buy or sell first. If you sell first, you don't have to carry two mortgages, you won't be in a rush, and you can negotiate from a position of strength. However, you may find yourself settling for a house that's less than ideal or, worse, entering the world of interim housing.

- Increase the saleability of your house by tidying up and depersonalizing, fixing obvious things, cleaning, getting a home inspection, and paying special attention to the lawn when selling in the summertime.

- Set the right asking price at fair market value – don't overprice or underprice your house.

- Recognize that realtors are worth the 5 or 6% commission they charge because they give valuable advice as to how best to get your house ready for sale and what the listing price should be, they list with MLS and can create a detailed marketing plan and brochures just for you, and they can negotiate impartially with potential buyers.

- Understand that selling your house yourself may be a false economy since you will have to do all the work a realtor does, and that you probably will not save the full commission since the buyer's agent needs to be paid, and that although discount realtors and unbundled services are available, you have to be vigilant as to agreements as to who does what — the savings may not be as great as you thought.

- Avoid such expensive mistakes as choosing the first realtor you meet, choosing the realtor who gave you the highest suggested listing price for your house, not paying attention to a proper marketing plan, not getting the house ready for sale, hanging around during initial showings and open houses, talking too much, and accepting a bad contingent sales offer.

Planning the sale carefully and making all the right moves can make a huge difference in the bottom line — how much money you get at the end of the day.

4

Renovations: Everything Old Is New Again

"Curtains in orange nylon and no place mats, there's not even the veneer of civilization."

— ALAN BENNETT

House renovation is a huge business in Canada. We spend about $2 billion each month on renovations and maintenance repairs to our houses. Deciding whether the renovations should be done and, if so, what should be done, how much should be spent, and when to do the work involves careful consideration. No one wants to spend money foolishly and it is therefore important to understand how this issue relates to your financial health.

There is much to consider before undertaking a renovation. This chapter reviews some of the key issues, such as how much to spend on what and when (i.e., is this a good time to install a gourmet kitchen?), and relates those issues to getting the most financial return on your house.

A Starting Point

The first thing to do is to consider whether or not it makes any financial sense to renovate, and, if it does, to decide what to do and when. The idea, of course, is to spend in such a way so as to be able to recover as much of the investment as possible at selling time or to increase the saleability of your house, all the while considering what is best for you and your family's lifestyle.

As mentioned earlier, Canadians spend a huge amount of money on renovations. Interestingly, renovation spending has been growing by leaps and bounds.

The amount of renovations that take place across Canada typically follows the housing market. In other words, as volumes of home sales increase, so does renovation spending. As you can see in the following chart, in the year 2001 there were just over 330,000 MLS sales, and, correspondingly, just under $25 billion in renovations. The more houses that change hands, the more people who want to personalize them.

Generally speaking, most people conduct renovations within the first three years of owning a home.[1] And given that most people sell their homes five to seven years after they buy, this means that most people do not renovate solely for purposes of adding value in a sale, but for lifestyle

Home Renovation Spending in Canada

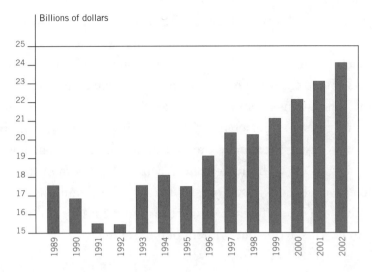

Sources: Canadian Real Estate Association; Statistics Canada CMHC Forecast 2001–2002.

Renovation Projects Generated by the Housing Market

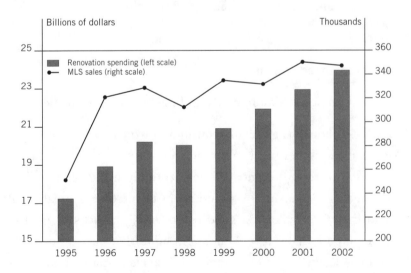

Sources: Canadian Real Estate Association; Statistics Canada CMHC Forecast 2001–2002.

considerations. You raise your family in the house, why not improve it to make it as comfortable as possible?

Improving saleability and generating a return on the investment is important, but so is timing. Doing a major renovation just before selling means not only that you may not get your money back, but also that you will not be able to enjoy the improvements. You have to decide why you are doing the renovations — strictly to make more money on the sale of the house or to get some personal satisfaction? Beware renovations that are dated in any way. For example are you planning to fill your house with "trendy" colours (as with the avocado-green appliances from the '70s)? Or make some big changes based on a style (as with the mirrored walls from the '80s)? Or will it be all right to enjoy the renovations for a couple of years and get some satisfaction out of them before selling?

Consider why people typically renovate.

1. It's an alternative to moving.

2. Rental property owners often renovate to keep or attract tenants.

3. Contractors and material are readily affordable.

4. Lenders have great deals for renovation loans.

5. Aging home needs repair.

6. Well-kept homes sell more easily and may be more valuable.[2]

A renovated house is generally considered worth more than one that is not. Most buyers do not want to do the work or may not have the time or the inclination to renovate and will pay a premium for a house that is in "mint" condition. Renovations would seem to increase the value of your house and therefore make it a good return on your investment. But you have to weigh potential return, keeping in mind that markets can go down — or go up — against your own personal financial situation. Does it make sense to borrow more money to increase the value? What are the current interest rates on loans? Are there any forecasts of housing prices for the next few years? There is no obvious dollar value for personal satisfaction, and you alone are the one to decide what the renovation is really worth to you. Generally, if you are going to enjoy the renovation *and* it is going to increase the value of your house, *and* the renovation is not so significant as to put the house out of character for the neighbourhood, then it does make sense to renovate.

Many studies have been done analyzing the impact certain renovations have on resale value. None of them suggests that any certain renovation, all else being equal, will generate a return greater than its cost, although some come close. It simply is not realistic to expect a future buyer to reward you on a dollar-for-dollar basis for the work you have done. That does not mean the work is not worth doing. There is nothing wrong with making the house just the way you want, but you won't get all the money back that you put into the renovation.

Occasionally, things are not equal and a renovation clearly makes sense. A good example of this is having a three-bedroom house in a neighbourhood of four-bedroom houses. If you have that problem, chances are yours will be a hard sell — the only way to sell it may be to reduce the price to reflect the fact that your house has that obvious defect that makes it inconsistent with all the others in the area. In that case, it makes good sense to look into a renovation that brings the house into the class or character of the neighbourhood. However, if you over-renovate, for example, by building an addition that makes the house much larger than those in the surrounding area, you may find that no one wants to spend your asking price and you may have to discount the house by the cost of the "excess" renovation.

Another example of when it makes sense to renovate before selling is when you have started renovations, but have not completely finished them. In touring the house, most buyers will notice only the uncompleted work, rather than placing value on what has already been done. For example, if you have renovated three out of the four bathrooms in the house, it probably makes sense to finish what you have started so that the house can be marketed as one that has all new bathrooms. The same holds true for landscaping the front yard but not the backyard. If you are going to sell your house (and ultimately everyone does), it makes sense to do both the front and back.

While a renovation may not give you a return on the investment greater than its cost, it is certain to facilitate a faster sale. Depending on the market, there is a real value in being able to sell your house when your neighbours are unable to sell theirs, which, in and of itself, is a sound reason for conducting the right improvements. Don't lose sight of the value in avoiding the stress of potentially carrying mortgages on two houses (as could be the case if you are unable to sell and have already purchased).

If you are considering whether to renovate before selling, it's a good idea to draw up plans and present them to an appraiser or a very knowledgeable realtor. He or she should be able to give you an idea of what the present value of your house is, then determine the renovation cost (add about 15% to their amount just to be safe) and the likely value of the house after the renovation. While this is no guarantee of what the value will be once you have done the work (market conditions can change quickly), it is a good indicator of the financial logic of the work. A good realtor or an appraiser should be able to point you to comparable houses in your neighbourhood that have sold recently and inform you a little about the condition of those houses so as to help you decide what should or should not be done.

Deciding To Renovate

If you have weighed the pros and cons of renovating and have decided to go ahead with it, it's interesting to look at the many available surveys that describe cost versus value for different renovations. The numbers do vary somewhat, perhaps due to flawed questions or regional variances. Regardless, the surveys are worth looking at closely.

Renovations To Do

In Canada, the Appraisal Institute has selected projects that their "specialists" feel offer the best potential for "payback" when selling. According to them, the average potential payback for different renovation projects is as follows:

- interior painting and décor — 73% of cost recovered;

- kitchen renovation — 72%;

- bathroom renovation — 68%;

- exterior painting — 65%;

- upgrading flooring — 62%;

- replacing windows or doors — 57%;

- main-floor family room addition — 51%;

- fireplace addition — 50%;

- basement renovation — 49%;

- furnace/heating system replacement — 48%.

The Ontario branch of the Appraisal Institute also produced some interesting numbers.

Average potential payback for renovations when a house is sold:

- kitchen — 78%;

- bathroom — 71%;

- interior painting — 74%;

- exterior painting — 63%;

- main floor family room addition — 55%;

- central air conditioning — 52%;

- new heating system — 50%;

- new windows — 48%;

- finishing the basement — 49%;

- landscaping — 35%;

- energy efficient features — 33%.

Studies in the U.S. on what payback will flow from renovations are also routinely done. One recent study showed the following average paybacks (assuming the house is sold within one year of doing the renovation):

- minor kitchen remodel — 88%;

- second-storey addition — 83%;

- bathroom remodel — 81%;

- bathroom addition — 81%;

- family room addition — 75%;

- master suite addition — 71%;

- major kitchen remodel — 71%.[3]

Another U.S. study showed the following:

- minor kitchen remodel — 94%;

- bathroom addition — 89%;

- major kitchen remodel — 87%;

- family room addition — 84%;

- two-storey addition — 84%;

- attic bedroom — 83%;

- master suite — 82%;

- bathroom remodel — 73%;

- siding replacement — 71%;

- deck addition — 70%;

- window replacement — 68%;

- home office — 64%.[4]

The numbers display some trends. It's obvious that some rooms are better to work on than others. Work done to kitchens and bathrooms are the clear winners from amongst the surveys. The rule of thumb is that the kitchen should be renovated if it is more than 20 years old and the bathroom should be renovated if it is more than 40 years old.

In working on kitchens or bathrooms, it is worth considering just how much renovation is necessary, since, as we've seen earlier, you probably won't get all your money back. Kitchen renovations generally start at about $10,000 — with the sky being the limit depending on your taste and the quality of what you install. Full kitchen renovations usually involve replacing the cabinets, flooring, countertops, and appliances. Bathrooms generally cost no less than $5,000 to do, although that number can increase dramatically if you have to relocate plumbing and wiring (and if you have expensive taste with regard to fixtures).

Renovations Not To Do

As we've seen, the most basic rule in the "reno" game is *not* to improve your house beyond the average for the area. People simply will not pay for unusual or over-renovated houses. And as we know, house prices are largely driven by their location. If you live in an area that is considered average — you may want to reconsider something such as a deluxe gourmet kitchen, since your selling price will likely not reflect the amount of money you spent on the fancy kitchen. The idea is that your house should "fit in" with the others in the area — not much nicer, not much worse. From an investment perspective, the last thing you want is to have the best home on the block; leave that to someone else. For example, if you live in a neighbourhood where most of the homes are single storey and you add a second-storey addition, you may actually lower the value of your house. The house may be out of character with the area — and if people in the area are looking for a certain type of house and yours doesn't fit in, then your value may be affected. On the other hand, having a new kitchen while others in the area have older ones will probably mean that you will sell your house faster and for more money than your neighbours. It's considered a good idea to visit open houses in your area to see the condition of your potential competition. You also want to keep track of which houses sell fast and try to figure out why.

The second most basic rule is that regardless of what you do, you should stick to styles that are classic. A renovation that is trendy or too stylish will only serve to limit the number of people who will find it appealing. The idea is to have an improvement that as broad a group of potential buyers as possible will find attractive. While you may find that boring, bear in mind that the point here is to conduct an improvement that will help sell the house, or strengthen its value. The best bet is to stick to light colours for the walls, carpets, and appliances. Avoid strong or dramatic colours in the house — they may limit the desirability of the house.

There are all sorts of renovations to beware of. For example, if you add a family room in the basement but your basement has a low ceiling, then it will not be something that many prospective buyers will value (especially if they have tall people in the family!). Similarly, a pool or spa may work for you, but many prospective buyers will not want to pay extra for the house just because it has those improvements. A pool, for example, may hinder the saleability of your home with some families, particularly those with small children, who might be more concerned about safety issues.

A renovation that is not professionally done is another thing to avoid. Unless it is your area of expertise, don't be tempted to "do it yourself." The time and effort, as well as the stress of trying to figure out how to do something correctly the first time, are simply not worth it. Not to mention the fact that the rules and regulations governing building standards change from time to time and you may not be aware of these changes. And the end result may not be quite what you had envisioned. Similarly, it's a good idea not to be cheap. The quality of the work you do should fit within the average for the area. If, for example, you renovate a basement but use very cheap flooring and don't bother with insulation in the walls, you may find buyers responding negatively when they realize that they may have to invest money to repair or upgrade what you have done.

Lastly, sacrificing one bedroom out of the total number of bedrooms in the house in order to make another one bigger does not make fiscal sense. The reason for this, again, has to do with the house being consistent with the average for the area. If you make it too unusual, you bear the risk of deterring potential buyers.

Inexpensive Improvements That Are a Good Return on Investment

There are many things you can do to improve the saleability of your house and increase its value, short of full renovation. Very often, it's not necessary to spend a lot of money fixing things up before a sale.

It may be that a minor remodel will be sufficient to decrease the time it takes to sell your house and recoup as much as possible from your investment. For example, in the kitchen, you could simply repaint the cabinets a light colour, replace the hardware, and drop in some nice shelf paper so that the kitchen has a fresh look to it. Updating the lighting fixtures is also a good idea. If you have a wood floor, consider sanding and refinishing it so that it looks new again.

In the bathrooms, the same rationale applies. Repainting and adding new hardware is relatively inexpensive, as is adding a new shower curtain. Another option to consider is reglazing the tub — that will make it look clean and shiny! Toilets and sinks are not expensive, and replacing the old ones can give the bathroom a "new" look.

Probably the best of the inexpensive fix-up options is simply to paint the house. If you are going to do this, remember that the general rule is to use colours as light as possible for the interior. (However, as shown below, the Appraisal Institute of Canada shows that non-neutral colours will be an upcoming trend. Although this may be a trend, I don't think it necessarily bodes well for future resale values.) Light colours have a way of making a house look bigger and certainly brighter. It's also easier for prospective buyers to picture their own things in your house when the colours are simple, clean, and light.

And the exterior paint job is probably even more important. You don't get a second chance to make a first impression and the first impression prospective buyers will get is from what they see when they first pull into your driveway. A new coat of paint will enhance the "curb appeal" of your house. While you are at it, be sure to manicure the landscaping, which will also add to the "curb appeal." Consider a new mailbox, outdoor light fixtures, and even a fancy door knocker — they will all be among the first things that get noticed.

Renovation Trends

In making decisions about renovating, an examination of the numbers as reported by existing studies can only take you so far. It's also a good idea to consider the trends. After all, if your goal is to try to make money or, at the minimum, make it so that your house will sell more quickly, why not try to anticipate what the demand will be for certain features as time goes on?

According to the Appraisal Institute of Canada[5], the top 10 upcoming renovation trends in Canada are:

1. main floor laundry room;

2. ground-floor home office;

3. hardwood flooring upgrade in kitchen;

4. whirlpool bath separate from the shower;

5. built-in kitchen appliances;

6. addition of kitchen cooking island;

7. non-neutral interior paint colours;

8. "smart" house wiring (wiring that allows for certain automatic functions, triggered by things such as motion, light, sound, time, or temperature);

9. home theatre room;

10. skylights.

When it comes to deciding what renovations to do, many homeowners ask themselves whether they will value the work done over the years. Will the renovation have "staying" power? Another issue to consider, especially if you are an aging baby boomer and think your house might appeal to other aging baby boomers, is whether the renovated house will contain the features that you or other aging boomers will value in the years to come. By the year 2017, almost half of all Canadians will be over 55 years old. Those people will need housing that offers features they value. Having a master bedroom on the first floor is also an appreciated trend, as is wider doorways so as to accommodate wheelchairs. If you are redoing a kitchen and bathroom anyway, why not construct the base cabinets so that they are removable, thereby allowing ease of access to those in wheelchairs? Some "trends" cost nothing and are always a good idea, such as placing electrical plug outlets 18 to 24 inches above the floor so that less bending is needed to access them. That sort of simple thing helps make the house appealing to older buyers. Similarly, when roughing in telephone lines, it's a good idea to add extra jacks in the family room to accommodate a monitored security system, as well as TV and phone jacks in all the bedrooms, which may be used by elderly parents who move in.

Some features of newly built homes offer guidance on this issue. After all, new home builders are keenly aware of what the trends are and follow them. Having a laundry room on the main floor, as a trend, comes as no surprise. With an aging population, who wants to drag the laundry all the way to a basement laundry room? The ground-floor home office also comes as no surprise. About 15% of Canadian households contain someone who operates a business from home.[6] Further, even for those who work out of the house, it is becoming increasingly common to have to take work home.

In a world that is becoming increasingly competitive, many people do extra work to stay ahead of competitors. There is an old, and truly unfortunate, saying that 9 to 5 is your job, but 5 to 9 is your career. Because of attitudes like that, creating a home office area is a sound choice.

Renovating with future trends in mind is not likely to create a positive and instant profit, but if you know you will eventually have to improve your house in order to sell, you might just as well do the improvements now that prospective buyers will likely find desirable. Even if you are not planning to sell for a few years, it makes sense to do the renovations and enjoy them for a while before selling. It is generally nicer to live in a renovated house than an unrenovated one; you may as well do the work right and enjoy it.

What Will It Cost?

As with anything, it helps to understand the "ins and outs" before starting a renovation. Obviously, you have to check out how much a renovation will cost before you can figure out how to finance it. Contractors are generally the ones people turn to for estimates and professional advice. The simplest starting point is to speak with a reputable general contractor who should be able to provide you with a ballpark estimate.

Dealing with Contractors

Not all contractors are the same and knowing how to best go about things can make a huge difference in the outcome of your renovation. The following are words to the wise.

Get written references.
Any contractors worth their salt will have the ability to produce several recent references from satisfied customers. If they cannot produce a written reference that is dated within the year, it is reasonable to assume that something must be wrong. It is also reasonable to ask for evidence of financial stability, such as a letter from the contractor's accountant or bank. The last thing you want is for the contractor to go bust in the middle of the job.

Check for insurance and licensing.

Your contractor should have a licence from the local licensing commission or trade or professional association. They should also carry liability insurance — public, general liability, and property damage — in an amount of not less than $1 million. It is also worth looking into your exposure to claims by workers injured on the job and to ensure that the contractor has appropriate protection that protects *you* against any claims by the contractors' injured workers.

Get it all in writing.

Once you have obtained two or three written estimates from different contractors, be sure to get the final deal in writing. It is important that you and the contractor are on exactly the same wavelength about the project. If there are structural changes, you will need drawings so that the contractors can bid on the same thing.

One of the oldest tricks in the contractors' book is for the contract not to specify absolutely everything. Then, as the job progresses, the contractor will point out that the deal did not include a specific item. The contractor knows that you cannot shop around for a fair price on the one item so they charge an artificially inflated price for the item. For example, the contract may refer to painting but not specify the number of coats or that a primer is needed. As the work commences, the contractor may come up to you and suggest an extra coat or a primer coat; you are then pretty much stuck. Remember — the contractor will only do what the contract requires him to do. One of the best ways to destroy your preplanned budget is to say to the contractor something like, "While you are at it, could you just do this little extra one thing?" That is music to contractors' ears. What appears minor to you may not appear so minor when you get the bill! If you have a budget and a contract, stick to it. Consider hiring an outside professional such as a design firm or even an architect to review the plans and contract and to advise you on whether or not they really include everything you need.

The contract should have some timing clauses, such as a start date, a finish date, and deadlines as to what has to happen when. Consider asking the contractor to put their money where their mouth is. I once asked a contractor how long he needed to get a certain job done. He instantly said that he needed four weeks. I asked him if he was prepared to agree to a contract that allowed him *six* weeks to do the work, but which would provide that the price of the job would decrease by 5% for every week that the work was not completed after the sixth week. He refused — and I did not hire him. Be sure to talk about payment: how much to pay and at what stages payment becomes due as the job progresses.

Also make sure that the contractor is in charge of applying for and obtaining all the necessary permits and that the contract states that all work will comply with applicable codes. You do not want to nor do you need to learn the minutiae of permit applications. That's best left to an expert. You also need to address municipal size and setback allowances. Again, this is best left to the designer, architect, or professional contractor. And always make sure to deal with the issue of who removes the debris — it can be surprisingly expensive! The contract should also contain all warranties and guarantees. Watch for these and be sure that it clearly states what is covered and the time it is covered for.

Familiarize yourself with your province's lien laws.

Each province except Quebec has a lien law. The law is designed to protect both the homeowner and subcontractors. You may be responsible if your contractor does not pay suppliers or workers who work on your job, and you can protect yourself by something called a holdback. The way it works is simple. Suppliers and workers only have a certain amount of time to register a claim for a lien on your property. You hold back payment in full (plus GST/HST) for that prescribed time and then pay the contractor in full only if no liens have been claimed. You can verify the lien issue by a quick search of your title. If a lien is there, you don't pay the holdback until it has been discharged. For this reason, it is wise to consult your real estate lawyer to find out what the rules are in your province as to the time frame and the holdback percentage. It is also a good idea to avoid clauses in the contract that obligate you to pay a certain amount on the contract regardless of lien claims. If the contractor tells you that they need a deposit so as to pay for supplies — consider making the cheque payable to both the contractor and the supplier. Any reputable contractor should have accounts with suppliers; if the contractor asks for too much of a deposit upfront, think of that as a red flag warning.

Avoid paying cash.

Anywhere from 40% to 55% of home renovations are paid for in cash. Generally, consumers do this in an attempt to get a better price by, for example, avoiding GST. Setting aside the legality (or illegality) of all this, there are some risks associated with paying cash that are worth considering.

The contractor may pocket the money, hiding it from the tax man and others. Not all contractors do this, but it is reasonable to operate on the assumption that a contractor demanding cash and offering no receipt is trying to dodge some obligations.

When you pay cash, you often do not obtain a record of payment. This can be a problem if the relationship between you and the contractor breaks down somewhere down the line. The contractor can deny you ever paid him and you may find yourself with a lien on your house as a result. If the contractor abandons the job partway through when you have paid him in cash, you might have no legal recourse (especially if you have no contract). If you must pay in cash, be sure to get a receipt. Otherwise, you might be faced with the daunting task of proving the contractor was even ever there.

The contractor who insists on cash may be unlicensed and uninsured. No studies have been done on this, but consider that there may be a greater chance that the sort of contractor who demands cash may be more likely to be the sort of contractor who cuts corners with the law — not being properly licensed or insured or neglecting to obtain proper permits. If any of those apply to your contractor, it spells trouble for you. For example, if a worker is injured while working on your house, you could be responsible. Paying cash to avoid tax is not legal and could prove to be a false economy — especially if something goes wrong.

To be fair, there are some very legitimate reasons for a contractor to ask to be paid in cash, particularly for small jobs. It may be that they are concerned that your cheque will not clear. It may also be that their bank "holds" money on deposit for a few days before allowing other cheques to be written against the funds on deposit. The bottom line is that while not all contractors demanding cash do so for nefarious reasons, it is worth protecting yourself when the situation arises.

Things To Watch Out For

The contracting industry certainly has its share of scams. If a contractor knocks on your door claiming to be working in the area and because of that is willing to offer you a "special" deal — beware. If they offer you a discount because they want to use your home to advertise — beware. If they ask for big, up-front deposits — beware. If the only address of the contractor is a post office box — beware. Inevitably, any scam will cost you more money than you originally prepared for. Generally, if something appears too good to be true, it probably is.

Financing the Renovation

Once you have satisfied yourself that you know what the renovation will cost, and consequently how much money you will need, it's time to go lender shopping.

When applying to a bank for a renovation loan, there are a few options. You can merely apply for a personal loan — take the money on deposit and then spend it as needed. If the amount of money you need is relatively small and you plan to repay it quickly, then the personal loan route may be the way for you to go.

Most of the time, however, people need more than just a small amount of money, making the personal loan route less than ideal. If your borrowing needs are more substantial (and that amount is all relative to your income, ability to repay, and budget), you may want to apply for a secured line of credit. The interest rate on a personal loan is higher than the interest rate on a loan that is secured by a mortgage. Moreover, when you borrow a lump-sum personal loan, you are paying interest on the entire amount, even though you don't really need to, since the money will likely be spent in bits and spurts, as you have to pay the contractor. In other words, if you don't need access to all the money at once, then it makes little sense to pay interest on money that is merely sitting idle in your account.

Applying for a secured line of credit is a better option for large amounts of money. This means that the bank agrees to lend you up to a certain amount and that debt is secured by a mortgage on your house. You draw only what you need — and thereby only pay interest as is absolutely necessary. You may even be able to access the line by a credit card! Secured lines of credit, especially those accessible via a credit card, are a popular product offered by lenders and are generally available at financial institutions.

In the approval process, the bank will look not only at your personal credit, but also at the house value to give them some comfort that the loan is not too risky. Once approved, you will be asked to sign a mortgage, which will be registered on your title. This process is much simpler today than it has been in the past and can be accomplished in as little as 24 hours. Once you have fully drawn the loan, the bank or other lender will likely offer you options to convert the debt into a conventional mortgage or blend it with your existing mortgage.

An option worth looking into is that of pre-approval. It's a good idea to go to your lender and find out in advance just how much money they are prepared to give you. Having that information will make planning the renovation that much easier.

Some people merely cash in their RRSPs to pay for a renovation. That can be a mistake and can generate unnecessary tax liability. Generally, the interest on the money you borrow for a house renovation is not tax deductible, meaning that you pay for it out of after-tax dollars. There are some creative ways to minimize the impact of that. For example, in what we will call scenario one, you could borrow against other investments you have, then have the investment make a loan to you (for the renovation).

Doing that will avoid some taxes, such as taxes you pay on cashing in an RRSP. (This issue is explored in more detail in Chapter 5.)

A second possible scenario would be to take out a line of credit with the investment funds as security. The loan payments can then be made using what is called a systematic withdrawal plan from your mutual funds. While the loan is not tax deductible, the funds invested stay within the mutual fund. Tax is generated only out of the money taken from the mutual funds to pay the loan.

For example,[7] say you have $100,000 invested in a non-registered account, in an international mutual fund with a cost of $65,000. If you amortize the loan over 20 years, with a rate of borrowing at prime plus one (assume 8%), your loan payment would be $538.43 per month. If your investment earned a return of 12%, at the end of 20 years your loan would be paid off and your mutual fund would be worth $469,350. The great thing is that the money you did not pay in lump-sum taxes continued to grow over a number of years. However, if you achieve more than the average return on funds, your return could well be in the area of 15% a year. Now look at what happens. The $65,000 loan is paid off and your investment at the end of 20 years is worth $922,117. You can be quite creative in how you finance renovations, but remember that this type of program for your investments is fairly complicated and you should have an experienced adviser to help you with all this.

Things To Keep in Mind

Renovating your house can be a rewarding step and can improve both the resale value and saleability of the property. As with so many other things in life, however, it's worthwhile doing your homework, researching the issue carefully before jumping in.

- Decide if it makes economical sense for you to renovate.

- If you decide to renovate, figure out when you are going to do it; generally speaking, it makes good sense to live in a renovated house for a couple of years and then sell, rather than making improvements just before selling.

- Figure out which renovations to do: studies have shown that kitchens and bathrooms give the most return for the money.

- Do not over-renovate or make your house unusual in any way.

- Some inexpensive improvements, such as painting and fixing the wiring, can be a great return on investment.

- Consider trends when renovating, such as putting a home office or a laundry room on the main floor.

- When dealing with contractors, make sure you get written references and check them out for insurance and licensing.

- Get their quotes for the job in writing, familiarize yourself with your province's lien laws, and, above all, avoid paying cash.

- There are a few options in financing a renovation, including personal loans, secured lines of credit, borrowing from your investments, or taking out a line of credit with the investment funds as security. Consider consulting with a financial adviser before proceeding to borrow money.

In renovating, there is a right time and a wrong time, renovations that will help you financially and ones that hurt you financially. Done right, a renovation can be a very smart move.

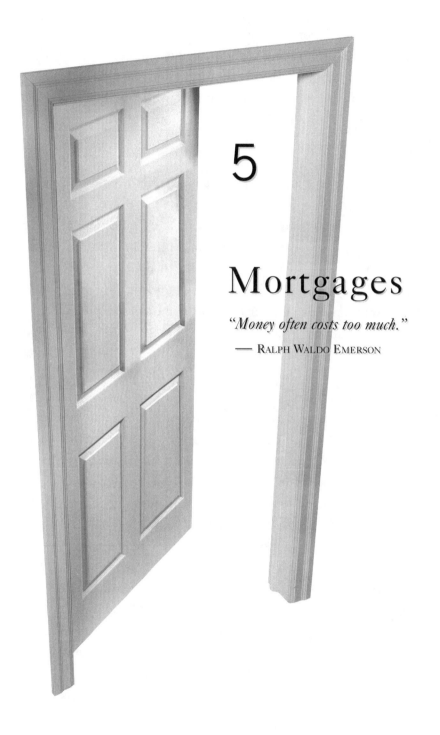

5

Mortgages

"Money often costs too much."

— RALPH WALDO EMERSON

The size of Canada's mortgage market is enormous. Two of every three households in our country own a home and one of every two of them has a mortgage. This translates into over three million outstanding residential mortgages at any given time, representing over $400 billion in debt! Over 40% of our GDP relates to outstanding housing loans.[1] No small wonder that Canadian lenders compete so fiercely for a crack at your business.

It used to be that there were very few choices in how you obtained a mortgage. You simply chose the bank you wanted to deal with, and, if you were approved, they would give you the mortgage. Today, lenders have demonstrated remarkable creativity in crafting different ways for you to borrow money. They have recognized that not everyone has the same needs and that to survive in a competitive environment they must determine all the different niches in the market and come up with products that match those individual markets.

The most obvious example of this is the "cash back" mortgage. Ten or so years ago, a banker would have been astonished by the suggestion that the bank, on funding a mortgage, would also give you a pile of money to spend as you will. Yet there are lots of people who could really use some extra money for things like furniture when they buy a house and the lender that made cash back popular also made a big dent in the market by offering that feature. Today, many lenders offer cash back on mortgage funding. In fact, that niche has spawned sub-niches, with lenders competing over the amount of the cash back and the terms attached to it. The point is that it is no longer safe to say that all mortgages are alike. There are many possible features to choose within a single mortgage, and the money you can lose from selecting the wrong mortgage can be significant. This chapter reviews mortgage basics, then delves deeper into the mortgage world with explanations of how best to deal with institutional lenders, the effect of different payment mechanisms, ways to pay off the mortgage sooner, and, lastly, unveiling the mystery as to how mortgage rates are established.

Mortgage Overview

Before you can consider any mortgage, you should have an idea of how much you want to spend on a house. A rough guideline as to approximately how much you should be spending on a house is to multiply your gross income by 2.2. From there you can determine how much of a down payment you will probably need and then go on to think about what lender you want to deal with and how to negotiate with this lender.

Types of Mortgages

It's helpful to know as much as possible about all the options available before you even go in to see the lender, including the main types of loans, as well as some of the basic features. The niches and features that lenders offer are all built on similar foundations, and it is essential to understand these various foundations.

Conventional Mortgage

A conventional mortgage is a first mortgage where the face amount is not greater than 75% of the value of the house. It is the most common type of mortgage. The value is usually determined by way of an appraisal process. The borrower must have the other 25% of the purchase price as a down payment or be able to raise those funds by way of a second mortgage (see below), which will stand second in priority to the conventional mortgage.

High-Ratio Mortgage

Banks do not lend beyond 75% of the house value without default insurance from either GE Capital (GE) or Canada Mortgage and Housing (CMHC), which protects them against the borrower defaulting on the loan. A high-ratio mortgage (also known as a default insured mortgage) is really just a conventional mortgage where the loan to value ratio is in excess of 75%. The lender must be an "approved" lender, although virtually every major lender is approved. The cost of the default insurance is typically added to the mortgage principal amount and varies based on the loan to value ratio —

generally not exceeding 3.75% of the loan for 95% LTV loans (for those who buy using the 5% down program.) A schedule of cost is available from GE Capital and CMHC (**www.gemortgage.ca** and **www.cmhc-schl.gc.ca**).

Open Mortgage

Mortgages that are truly open carry no restrictions: you can pay them off at any time without penalty. Unfortunately, most mortgages that are described as open actually are only "sort of" open. Regardless of the moniker, most open mortgages do have mechanisms that allow for early payout with little or no penalty — making them an ideal choice for those who value or require the flexibility of paying off the mortgage quickly, such as upon a sale of the house. In part because the lender does not enjoy the certainty that the loan will be outstanding for a length of time, rates for open mortgages are generally a bit higher than for closed mortgages.

Closed Mortgage

Closed mortgages involve unchanged payments for a predetermined obligatory term. The term can vary, but you are locked in for that term. You cannot discharge your mortgage when you sell during the term without getting the lender's consent, which carries a price tag (namely a penalty). This can be a good choice if you have no plans to sell during the term, because closed mortgages generally carry lower interest rates than open mortgages. As with open mortgages, closed mortgages are frequently not truly closed — there are some prepayment privileges involved, allowing you to pay off a portion of the principal annually.

Fixed-Rate Mortgage

A fixed-rate mortgage is just that; one where the interest rate is predetermined. During the term, you will always pay the same amount towards the principal and interest on the loan. This is a nice feature for those who prefer to budget precisely.

Variable-Rate Mortgage

When you select this type of mortgage, the interest rate that you pay fluctuates with the market. Your payments stay the same — what changes is the internal allocation of the money by the lender. If, for example, interest rates rise, then the portion of your payment that goes towards the interest increases. At the same time, your amortization period also goes up. That means that while you have a deal to pay the same monthly amount, the length of time it would take to completely pay off the debt increases, because your payment cannot change, but the interest rate has.

Conversely, if rates have fallen since you first took out your variable rate mortgage, your payments remain the same, but the amount that goes towards principal reduction is increased and the amortization period is decreased. The mortgage will be fully paid off in a shorter time frame than you originally contemplated when the loan first was placed. That, of course, can change too — if rates rise again.

The nice thing about a variable rate is that it means your mortgage is always reflective of the state of the market; you will never be stuck paying off more to the interest when the interest rates are low, and vice versa. In choosing between fixed-rate or variable-rate mortgages, you are really choosing between the security of the fixed rate and the risk of the varied rate: you might save money (if rates fall) or spend more (if rates rise) with the varied rate. With a fixed-rate mortgage, the amount of your payment that goes towards principal reduction and interest is predetermined. Regardless of whether rates rise or fall during the term, everyone is obligated to the original deal. The winds may shift in the lender's direction or in yours. With a variable-rate mortgage, you are essentially shifting the risk of financial loss or gain due to changes in the market interest rate during your mortgage term from the lender to yourself. Therefore, the rate may be lower (although not by much) so as to compensate you for that risk.

Convertible Mortgage

This type of mortgage allows you to lock in during the term to a longer-term mortgage. It usually is for six months to one year and carries rates that are similar to short-term closed rates. If you feel rates are on the rise, you merely agree to change to the longer-term commitment. With this type of mortgage, you get the benefit of the better rate for the closed term with the flexibility of protecting yourself if you see rates rising.

Portable Mortgage Feature

When you are first applying for a mortgage — any kind of mortgage — one feature that is extremely important to ask about is the portable feature. This feature allows you to transfer (or "port") a mortgage from one property to another, so long as you maintain the original loan amount or increase the loan and stay with your original lender, without penalty. People don't generally plan to sell their house in the middle of the mortgage term, although something may happen that makes selling logical. Usually, people sell and buy another house while still maintaining or increasing the amount of the mortgage. Banks charge penalties for early mortgage discharges based on their "losing" the loan. If you have the portable feature and then sell and buy and maintain or increase the debt, then the bank is not really losing a loan — they are transferring their security from one property to another.

From a legal perspective, the mortgage on the house you are selling is actually paid off and the mortgage is discharged from title, with a brand new mortgage being placed on the property you are buying. This is done because the buyer of the property you are selling is entitled to acquire title free and clear of your mortgage. The "port" is really only an internal bank type of thing — designed to minimize or eliminate penalties. However, it's important to realize that this is one of those features that you need to ask about; if you don't, it could cost you money in penalties to pay out the mortgage prematurely upon a sale.

Self-Directed RRSP

There is a way for you to hold your mortgage within your RRSP, thereby allowing you the luxury of essentially paying yourself the interest on the mortgage, instead of paying it to a lender. This involves some know-how and expense to set up and consumers are well advised to seek professional advice.

Best Ways To Shop for a Mortgage

As I said at the beginning of the chapter, having the right mortgage is crucial for getting the most out of your house. And having the right mortgage involves getting the right lender. How you shop for a mortgage can affect the financial outcome of your purchase.

The Application

The first thing to do when shopping for a mortgage is positioning your application so that it fits the lender's ideal criteria.

When you apply for a loan to buy or refinance a home, the lender typically considers two issues in deciding whether to accept your application and, if so, on what terms: your previous repayment habits and the value of the property in question. At the risk of stating the obvious, the lender wants some comfort that if they lend you money, you will pay it back. A credit check is done to give the lender a feel for your past habits of paying bills. If you have no credit history, there is nothing for the lender to base a decision on and you may be declined for that reason alone. If you have never borrowed money before and want to buy a house and obtain a mortgage, it is a good idea to establish a credit history. This is easy — all you need to do is obtain a credit card and make sure you make payments on time. Another option is to borrow for an RRSP, again making sure you make all payments on time. RRSP loans are reasonably easy to obtain because their proceeds are used to buy an asset that, in turn, forms some security for the lender.

Before Shopping

Before shopping for a house or mortgage, it is a good idea to get a copy of your credit report from the local credit bureau and check to see if it is accurate. And don't be alarmed if it isn't. It's not unusual for there to be mistakes on the report, so it's wise to get the report a few months in advance of your entry into the house or mortgage market to allow enough time to correct any errors. On the report, you will see a number beginning with an "R," which reflects your past payment patterns for rotating credit, like a credit card. It's considered rotating since you can charge to it and repay it and charge again all within the same month. If you have paid the debt off or have made the minimum payment as it became due, then you are considered an R1. If you are three months behind, you are considered an R3. The higher the number, the worse things get. If you see an R9, it means that the lender has written off your loan. If you have any installment loans, the letter "I" will appear before the number.

Remember, the lender will look at the credit report and if it contains inaccuracies, then you may find your loan application denied for that reason alone.

It's also a good idea to pay off credit card or other charge card privileges (such as department store cards) before shopping for a house or a mortgage. This has the effect of making you appear "cleaner" or in better financial health to a prospective lender.

You should also have an idea of what you can afford. If you know the price range of the type of house you would really like, but perhaps don't have access to a lot of funds for a down payment, take a look at the various government programs designed to help people enter the housing market. I believe that if the government has the decency to create such programs, the least you could do is take them up on their offer. The 5% Down program (essentially default insurance through either GE Capital or CMHC) has helped thousands of Canadians enter the housing market. It is even possible today to buy a house with 100% financing (conditions apply). The feds also allow you to borrow from your RRSP under their Home Buyers Plan (conditions apply). Further, new homes are eligible for a partial rebate of the nasty GST, and some provincial governments have programs that allow for a waiver of the property or land transfer tax to certain eligible first-time buyers. Educate yourself or seek professional advice and find out what programs the government has crafted that help you.

Lastly, consider getting a mortgage pre-approval before shopping; it will tell you exactly how much money you have to spend and provides protection against rate increases for 60 days. While the pre-approval lets you know what you have to play with, it does not obligate you to actually go through the transaction with that lender.

Rules Lenders Live By

As with so many things in life, there are rules, more rules, and then some (we will not get into the forms yet). Tied into your credit rating are guidelines that tell lenders how much of a loan you should have. Major lenders typically require that the total of all you plan to spend on mortgage principal, mortgage interest, taxes on the home, and heating be no more than 32% of your gross monthly income. That amount, plus whatever you spend on other debt payments (like car loans and credit cards) cannot be more than 40% of your gross monthly income. Want to impress your banker? Let them know that you understand their lingo. The 32% rule is called the GDS — Gross Debt Service ratio. The 40% rule is called the TDS — Total Debt Service ratio. Unless you comply with both these rules, lenders, especially major ones, are not likely to accept your application.

The second thing lenders look at is the value of the property you want the mortgage placed on. The lender wants to be sure that the house value is greater than the amount of the mortgage. As we saw in the discussion about high ratio mortgages, lenders are not supposed to lend you more than 75% of the value of the property without obtaining default insurance. They determine that value by an appraisal. There are several kinds of appraisals, which vary in price. These range from electronic computer valuations (which are now available in many parts of Canada), to drive-by viewings, to full inspections of the property. The lender will choose the right appraisal for your deal based upon their experience with loans such as the one you are seeking. For instance, if you are borrowing what the lender considers to be a large amount of money, they will send out a professional appraiser to figure out the value of the property through a full inspection. They may do this with new home construction, too, since they may not want to rely upon purchase price alone to determine the home's value.

It's important to remember that both credit and value have a lot to do with not only whether you will be approved, but also at what rate. If your credit is poor, but you are only borrowing a small amount in relation to the property value, you may be approved anyway. Similarly, if your credit rating is good, but you don't comply with the TDS/GDS rules, you may be declined.

Banks like rules. It makes their lives easier. They breed predictability. Like it or not, you are better off trying to work with their rules (after all, it is their money). Understanding the issues that the banks rules contend with and complying with what the banks call "standard lending criteria" will only increase your chances of coming out with the best deal for you.

The Internet

The Internet is a gold mine of information and can be a great place to start learning about mortgages. Checking the daily posted rates is easy — just click onto any bank Web site or one of the sites listed in the index, which provides a spreadsheet of posted rates. You'll see that there are some differences among the different institutions as to what they post. The bank-posted rates tend to be higher than some of the credit unions or online virtual or branchless lenders.

Secondary lenders such as smaller financial institutions may also post rates different than the pack, but, remember that they may have different lending criteria. Watch what you are comparing. Few people pay the banks' posted rates since it is normal to obtain some sort of reduction or an enhanced package, while the online or discounters have already lowered their rates. Be sure you are comparing the best rates each institution offers with one another and be keenly aware of the big difference the terms of the loan (such as prepayment privileges and portability) have on your individual situation. Rates are important — but should not be the sole consideration in selecting a lender. The Internet is a great place to start, and it is possible to get a mortgage loan online, but almost no one does, most preferring at some point to deal with a good old-fashioned human being.

Canadian use of the Internet is much different when it comes to mortgage shopping as opposed to house shopping. Over two-thirds of wired Canadians will look to the Internet to help them shop for a house,[2] while about one-third of Canadians will look to the Internet to help them shop for a mortgage.[3]

While 33% of Canadians will look to the Internet for information about mortgages, only about 4% will pre-qualify online and a mere 1% will actually apply for a loan online.[4] This proves that efficiency by way of technology does not always alter consumer shopping patterns. People like to deal with people, especially when it comes time to discussing and negotiating a mortgage.

Banks, mortgage brokers, realtors, and sites like Homestore, Homeadvisor, Etrade, Canoe, Quicken, and others offer loads of useful information. (see Appendix 1.)

Bank or Mortgage Broker?

Most transactions originate in one of two ways. People either apply directly to a lender or they work through a mortgage broker. It is not correct to say that one route is better than the other. Rather, the thing to do is to understand the differences between the two processes and choose the one that best suits your financial needs. There are differences between how the two work.

Banks sell loans and, as sellers, it is not unreasonable for them to try to get the best deal they can so as to maximize the return they offer their shareholders. Loans are part of their day-to-day business. With a bank, you deal directly with the entity lending the money.

Brokers do not sell loans — they sell service (trying to get the best mortgage on your behalf). If their service were no different from that of the banks, then there would be no reason for them to exist. Whichever route you choose, it is possible for you to obtain inexpensive professional advice on selecting the product that suits your individual situation best.

A mortgage broker will assess your needs and try to place your loan on your behalf. The broker may use a "bid" system, in which the broker electronically submits an application to a number of lenders at the same time. The lenders, who may pay the broker a fee for placing the mortgage, then have the opportunity to view your loan needs and bid on the loan. Participants in the "bid" system usually include the major banks, but lenders that are considered secondary also join them. A secondary lender will typically be a life insurance company or smaller trust company, which may have looser lending criteria than some of the major lenders and may therefore accept loans that major banks decline, although potentially on different terms. The lenders on the system will ordinarily respond within four hours of receiving the application. As a consumer, you then go back to the mortgage broker's office to see who bid on your loan.

If the broker is unable to place your loan in the primary market (chartered banks and trust companies), they may resort to what is known as "private money." Those are funds of other individuals who are looking for loans to place. If your broker places your loan in the "private" market, you will typically pay interest at a rate higher than that posted by the banks, as well as fees to the broker on closing (but if your loan is placed with the primary banks, those banks ordinarily pay the broker). While the "loan" will cost you more, that may be your only option.

Mortgage brokers work on a commission basis; they tend to be highly motivated and will work hard to get their customers a good deal. A mortgage broker is on your side of the fence — they work for you. Because they are so motivated, brokers will usually arrange appointments at times convenient to their customer, and you can often get them to visit you in your office or in the evening at your home, if necessary. Brokers typically have knowledge of the nuances of the various banks offerings. They can apply their expertise to your needs, following an assessment of what is best for you. In all fairness, good bankers can do the same thing, but the bankers will only have knowledge of the products that their particular bank offers.

Current estimates indicate that mortgage brokers originate about 25% of all new mortgages in Canada.[5] This number is on the rise, and some people suggest that this number will grow dramatically over the next few years to the point where the majority of Canadians will be using mortgage brokers as more foreign and online lenders, who do not have a bank network, enter the market and seek distribution channels. Although changes in shopping patterns tend to evolve slowly, I believe some increase in the use of mortgage brokers is a virtual certainty. I also believe that more major lenders will look to brokers as an efficient source of new bank business and that practice will also grow over time.

While consumer use of independent brokers is a growing trend in Canada, the reality is that the vast majority of consumers apply directly to a lender such as a bank. Banks have responded to the clear consumer need to have mortgage services available in a convenient manner via increased branch hours and have also brought in "floating" mortgage representatives. The floating reps, sometimes called mortgage development officers, work a lot like brokers, offering levels of service that rival those of independent mortgage brokers, and are often paid on a performance basis. Because of these new developments, it is no longer true that the only way to get a mortgage from an "A" lender, like a chartered bank, has to involve a trip to the local branch of the bank during office hours. It's also untrue that a mortgage broker will always, by necessity, get you a better deal. The outcome often has to do with your negotiating skill and/or current bank promotions.

Some people simply like to have a live person to talk to when borrowing money. When you use a broker, you do not always get to actually meet a representative from the lender. Some people care about that and others don't see the value in building a relationship with a representative of the lender. It is simply a personal preference.

The nice thing about all this is that choice and competition invariably produce one winner — the consumer — who gets increased service levels at lower rates.

Bank Pointers

Since mortgages have become such an increasingly competitive game, it has almost come to the point where banks don't make money through mortgage offerings, but instead hope to leverage the relationship they have established with you for other business. If you have other business, such as an RRSP, credit card, savings, and chequing account or small business account, then it makes sense to present your mortgage application as a package. This means negotiating with the lender (banker) so that if they offer a good rate on a mortgage, the institution will also get your business for:

- personal savings account;

- personal chequing account;

- RRSP;

- credit cards;

- kids' savings account;

- RESP (Registered Education Savings Plan);

- business account;

- car loan;

- life insurance on the mortgage.

There is no magic in negotiating with a bank for the best deal. You are best off simply letting the banker know that you will be shopping around and asking them to give you their best shot. You need to be aware of the various mortgage options, since the best rate on a mortgage does not necessarily translate into the best deal for you. (The mortgage could have poor prepayment privileges or no portability, both of which can cost a lot of money if you want to prepay but cannot, or want to sell and get stuck with a penalty.) However, most people do shop by rates. Packaging your business can help you because the bankers know that they will make money on your other business and can then afford to let loose a bit on the mortgage. The idea is to give them the business you need to have a bank do anyway. Even if you don't get a fabulous mortgage rate deal, they may offer advice on what can be done to your overall financial health once they see what you have in your package. The bankers' advice can range from more efficient borrowing methods for other business to something as simple as waiving service charges on your other accounts if you give them your mortgage.

Mortgage Broker Pointers

Brokers are performance-driven. They only make money if they get your deal. That means that time is of the essence for them. It's important to recognize this when dealing with them and to have what they will need ready. In visiting a broker, always have the following with you:

- agreement of purchase and sale (unless you are pre-qualifying);

- latest tax return;

- pay stub (or a letter from your employer confirming income);

- list of assets;

- list of liabilities.

What Not To Do When Shopping or Before Closing

When shopping for a mortgage, it's important to be aware of your overall financial health as never before. Sometimes, totally innocent acts can have dire consequences. The reality is that there are things you can do that can sabotage your chances of getting a good deal on your mortgage.

Don't Request Your Credit Rating Too Many Times

As we saw earlier, one of the first things a lender will do when you apply for a mortgage is check your credit rating. Your credit report will not only outline your various debt payment habits, but will also assign you a number (and you thought you weren't a number!), called a Beacon Score. This number gives the lender some guidance as to what you have been like when it comes to borrowing and repaying. Beware! That score is adversely affected by the number of times someone requests a score (which can happen, for example, if you shop around for a mortgage with a variety of lenders within a 10-day window of each other). The computer that generates the number operates on the assumption that many people seeking credit reports means something negative is going on and reflects that adverse inference in the end score. I'm not sure the machine is correct in that assumption, but, regardless of what I think, shopping around too much may just backfire as a tactic for getting the best deal.

Don't Buy a Car

When lenders look at your application, they are required to examine how much debt your income can support. They are bound to follow guidelines (see above on the subject of TDS/GDS). Car payments are factored in. The money you spend on car payments is money you do not have available for mortgage payments. Figure out what that money buys you in increased house shopping dollars. A $400 per month car payment that is avoided can buy you over $55,000 in house shopping dollars through a mortgage!

The period of time between mortgage approval and the actual funding date or closing is a very, very bad time to buy a car. If you do, and the lender finds out, you may lose your mortgage. This is especially so if the car loan alters your debt service ratio (TDS/GDS) such that you fall outside what the bank's parameters are. The same rationale holds true for new credit cards or, for that matter, any major credit purchases, such as furniture. It is not uncommon for people to buy a house and get a mortgage approval, and then go on a shopping spree before closing for new furniture, car, and more only to find out shortly before closing that the lender has backed off on the mortgage approval because too much debt has been taken on.

Don't Forget To Ask About Fees

Just because you are approved for a $100,000 mortgage does not mean that you will actually get a cheque for $100,000. The lender may deduct fees for various items including appraisal, default insurance application, and more (which, for a $100,000 mortgage could be around several hundred dollars). Be sure to ask how much the cheque your lawyer gets will be for.

Don't Quit Your Job or Change Jobs

Lenders do not like instability. They like to see a stable track record of earnings and employment. If you change jobs before you apply for a mortgage, you may be declined for that very reason alone as the lender may require a certain period of time with one employer as part of their "standard" approval process. Changing jobs creates, in the lender's mind, a very legitimate concern about your future earnings.

And, as with buying a car above, one of the worst things you can do is to change jobs after the approval but before the closing of your mortgage. Some lenders check with your employer before they make the advance of the mortgage. If they do that and you are no longer there, you may well have the mortgage commitment cancelled at the very last minute. If you are employed and are thinking about starting your own business and becoming self-employed, you are well advised to wait until after you get the mortgage before making such a move. (And even then, you may want to wait to see how the mortgage payments are affecting your lifestyle before making such a big change.)

Don't Be Sold Too Quickly

Banks often have promotions in an attempt to get your business. Some of them are catchy and appear to be great deals. They may well be — or it may be that another deal works out better for you. Consider that all deals from all banks are quantifiable (have a dollar value). Again, prepayment privileges and portability features add up, and the deals that include these features are worth more than those that do not. In assessing the various options, it helps to try to sort out the real bottom-line value.

Don't Make a Decision Without Professional Advice

Many people already view home ownership or the refinancing process as a legitimate part of their overall financial plan — which only makes good sense. If the mortgage is part of your overall financial plan, then logic dictates that you would consult your financial planner prior to making a decision on something as major as a mortgage. One of the nice things the planner will do is provide you with impartial advice on which option is better for you. The planner is probably the only expert on mortgages who can provide you with truly impartial advice. The people at the lending institutions have a vested interest in what you choose to do (they want to sell you something). Even mortgage brokers can be swayed, since some lenders pay them more for promoting certain products. The planner can help you figure out what the bottom-line cost is for the mortgage offering you are considering.

Having said that, don't lose sight of the fact that some of the offerings have values in and of themselves that, while quantifiable, offer certain advantages that may be of more value to you than other people. For example, cash back comes in handy to help buy furniture. A deep discount in the first year comes in handy when your cash flow may be weakest, having just bought a house. The essential thing here is to make an informed decision. For example, many consumers value a 3% cash-back offer more than a 1% discount, yet any planner will tell you that you are better off in the long run with the 1% discount — you pay less interest that way! In choosing the mortgage that is best, consumers also place value on such unquantifiable factors as the speed of the loan decision process and a lender who takes care of their needs and makes them feel valued.

Second Mortgages

There are times when it makes sense to have two mortgages on your house
— a first and a second. Second mortgages are typically arranged on
purchases as a manoeuvre to avoid paying default insurance premiums.
Here's how it works: when you buy a house and have less than a 25% down
payment, you end up paying insurance against default (available from GE
Capital and CMHC only) so that the bank can lend you more than 75% of
the house value. The amount of the premium (plus tax in many parts of
Canada), which is a one-time payment, is on a sliding scale and can be as
much as 3.75% of the mortgage amount. If you have the ability to regularly
pay down the mortgage quickly, it can make sense to have a first mortgage
of 75% and a second for what you need beyond that (although only up to
90% of the house value), and not pay the default insurance. The second
mortgage will be at a higher rate of interest, but if you truly believe you can
pay that off quickly, you may be financially better off going the second-
mortgage route.

The only way to truly assess this issue is through analysis. Most people
will need some expert advice on this issue, which is readily available from
your banker, mortgage broker, or financial planner, any of whom will be
happy to assist you in the calculation. The key in the calculation is the
amount of time you really need, considering your overall finances, to pay
down or eliminate the second mortgage. If you can withstand some short-
term pain, you may wind up saving a lot of money!

Sometimes, second mortgages can be used as a way to get some extra
cash. For example, if a house is worth $200,000 and you have a first
mortgage of $125,000 and you need an extra $40,000, you have a couple of
choices. You can increase the amount of the first mortgage or you can apply
for a second mortgage. If you choose to get a second mortgage (and are
approved), the bank places a second charge on the property when they
advance the loan. When the property is sold, both mortgages have to be
paid out. If you default on the second mortgage, then the lender can
exercise their rights as a power of sale and sell the house, then use the

proceeds (after expenses) to pay off the first mortgage. If there is anything left, then the second mortgage gets paid.

The Sub-Prime Market

Not everyone gets approved for a mortgage when they apply. But being declined by a bank doesn't necessarily mean an end to your dream of home ownership. All it means is that your application falls outside something known as "standard lending criteria." And it also doesn't mean that you are a bad person or even a bad risk. All it means is that you do not fall within the four corners of the system devised by banks to semi-automatically adjudicate loan applications. You may well be declined due to a previous bankruptcy (despite current high income), self-employment (despite a successful enterprise), new immigrant status (despite possession of significant equity), or a life event like divorce, resulting in credit failure. This segment of the mortgage market is known as the "sub-prime" portion, or "B," "C," and even "D" loans. In the U.S., the size of the sub-prime market has been estimated at about 10% of all mortgages. Canadian estimates are at about 15%.

If you are declined by an "A" lender, do not despair; there are other options. A good broker may place you with secondary lenders such as some of the trust companies who often have looser lending criteria. You may wind up with a lender such as XCEED Mortgages (owned by the Bank of Montreal), which specializes in sub-prime lending, or others, such as First Line Trust, or your broker may place your loan in the private mortgage market (individual investors who buy sub-prime first and second loans). The interest rate you pay is dramatically higher than with an "A" lender and you will likely have to pay steep fees (which can be added to the loan), but at least you get the loan and can enter the real estate market.

Prudent buyers who are forced into the sub-prime market are well advised to go short (see below) on their mortgages. The idea is that after a year or two of regular payments, you may no longer be considered sub-prime by the "A" lenders. Once that happens, you can apply to refinance the property at regular rates.

Long or Short?

Buying a new home means having to make some tough decisions, the results of which can have a significant impact on your financial health. One of the many things you have to decide in the course of the home-buying process is choosing the length of term of your mortgage. There are various options available and much to consider.

In order to make this decision, you need to know the difference between the mortgage's term and the amortization period. The amortization period is the length of time it would take to pay off the mortgage completely. Lenders use the amortization period (ordinarily 25 years) as a basis to calculate payments during the term. Regardless of the term, if you have a 25-year mortgage amortization, that means that if you made your payments regularly and identically for 25 years, the mortgage would be paid off.

The term of the mortgage is the length of time you borrow money from a lender. When the term is up, your mortgage is due, meaning you have to either renew it or pay it off. You can pay it off with your own money or with money from another mortgage with a different lender. Thus, the term is a portion of time within the amortization period. For example, if you have a 5-year term on a new mortgage with a 25-year amortization, that means that after 5 years, you still have 20 years of payments left.

Short-term mortgages generally have a term of less than 3 years; long-term mortgage terms are usually 3 to 10 years. In most cases, short-term mortgages have lower interest rates than long-term ones. The downside of a short-term mortgage is that it does not offer you the security that the long-term option does in the sense of knowing for a long time what your monthly mortgage payments will be.

Deciding whether to "go short" or "go long" can be a tough decision. The overriding factor really has to do with your appetite for risk. If you are the sort who can afford to take chances, and if you have a fair amount of equity in your house, you may be better off going for a short-term mortgage. If, on the other hand, an increase in your monthly mortgage payment budget would be financially devastating, then you probably should go for a long-term mortgage. You will likely pay a bit more, but at least you will know what the monthly payments are going to be and can budget for them.

Keep this in mind: If you think interest rates are going down, then you might be better off going short to take advantage of lower rates at renewal time. If you think rates are going to go up, then you might be better off locking in. It's always a good idea to have a close look at the spread between short- and long-term rates. In some markets, the spread can be significant, while in others, the spread may not be all that much. If the spread is not significant, then you might value the flexibility of a shorter-term mortgage.

Many lenders offer hybrid products — mortgages that, for example, combine the benefit of the lower rate of a short-term option, but that allow you to lock in if rates start to rise. These are worth considering.

No one has a crystal ball that can definitively tell you what's best. It's important, though, to understand all the options so as to make an informed decision.

For what it's worth, history has shown that people who have gone "short" in the last few years saved a pile of money. A recent study by Dr. M. Milevsky of York University in Toronto concluded that 88.6% of the time over the past 15 years, consumers would have saved money borrowing at prime (short rate) versus a five-year fixed rate. According to the study, "There is no reliable predictor of where rates will go, so consumers are better off not guessing and just going with a floating rate."[6] Milevsky stands by his statement, even after factoring in typical rate discounts generally available in recent years. Simply put, those who want the security of a fixed long-term payment on their mortgage end up paying for that privilege. However, the study notwithstanding, a long-term fixed rate still makes sense for those who cannot tolerate fluctuations in their monthly mortgage payment.

The Renewal Market

Practically all of the advice offered in this chapter is as relevant to the renewal process as it is to the process of getting a mortgage when buying. Those who are renewing mortgages represent the largest part of the mortgage market. Many lenders choose to focus their marketing efforts on smaller portions of the market, such as first-time buyers, and do not bother too much with renewals, figuring that renewers will likely not bother switching. And, in fact, experience has shown that rationale to be correct. I believe that will change in the near future. Switching lenders is remarkably simple and inexpensive. Because the process has become so simple, it's a fair bet that you will begin to see lenders increase marketing efforts around renewals, in an effort to attract new business away from their competitors.

Borrowers in general do show a high degree of loyalty to their existing lender, and they often renew simply on the strength of their lender's initial offer without shopping around for reasons that may be nothing more than convenience. This, of course, ignores the value in shopping around. For some strange reason, many borrowers are under a false impression that switching lenders at renewal time is a big deal. Because of that, a surprising amount of people end up paying posted rates for their mortgage on renewal, not realizing that shopping around or even asking for a sharper deal will often result in dramatic cost savings.

But improvements in technology and title insurance have changed the dynamic of the renewal market. Today, some people are keeping their eyes open for any deal, and some borrowers will switch lenders for as little as 1/4% interest saved.   Shoppers keen on getting the best deal will begin looking around a few months before their mortgage matures. You should approach the renewal process in much the same way as you would approach the process of arranging the mortgage when buying a house. Shop around. At the minimum, you want to determine whether or not the renewal offer you have received is the best deal you can get.

When shopping around to see if another lender would be interested, you can apply for a pre-approval directly to a lender or even work with a mortgage broker on the deal. From a process perspective, if you are not increasing the amount you owe the lender, you merely need to have the new lender do a "switch," which is an assignment of the existing mortgage from one institution to another. An amending agreement is then signed, outlining the new deal you have. No new mortgage is registered on your title — the new lender merely relies on the existing registration, plus the amending agreement, which is then registered on your title. Because of the simplicity of the process, the cost is usually minimal or nothing.

Default insurance on your mortgage is also transferable when switching lenders and generally at no cost!

If you are increasing the amount owed under the mortgage, the process is a bit different. In that case, the old mortgage must be discharged and a new one placed. That process, which used to take up to two weeks, is much simpler today and can be accomplished in some parts of Canada on a same-day basis. The cost of discharging the old and placing a new mortgage on title has also dropped significantly over the past several years, due to technology and title insurance. Some consumers are able to negotiate having the new lender absorb this cost as part of the overall deal. Don't forget that the lender will likely also require an appraisal if the amount owing is being increased.

While the process of switching or refinancing has become efficient and less costly, that does not mean that there will not be any expenses. If you are looking at refinancing in the middle of the term of your existing mortgage, you will have to consider the issue of penalties. These vary based on the difference in market interest rates between your existing mortgage and the one you are considering. That difference is known as the Interest Rate Differential. Simply put, the interest rate differential is the difference between the rate you have on your current mortgage and the rate on the new one, multiplied by the sum owing. Many lenders simplify this process by imposing a minimum three-month penalty. While the penalty can be steep, sometimes it makes sense to pay it anyway — especially if current rates have dropped significantly below what you have been paying. A good financial adviser, banker, or broker will be easily able to work out a calculation of total interest for you so as to demonstrate when, in your situation, it makes sense to break the existing mortgage, pay the penalty, and get a new one at a lower rate. Try your existing lender first. That lender will be able to blend the penalty in with the new mortgage; you may end up with a lower overall payment that will not be as low as what it could be, but you will avoid paying a lump sum penalty.

The general rule of thumb is that in order for it to make financial sense to pay a penalty and lock in on a longer term at a lower rate, the rate differential has to be significant and you should have more than 18 months left on your existing mortgage.

A final word of warning: If you have had trouble maintaining regular mortgage payments on time or if the value of your house has dropped, you may find yourself with no alternative but to deal with your existing lender. Other lenders may not want you because of a credit problem. If the value has dropped, you may find yourself having to buy default insurance upon refinancing.

Tips To Pay Off That Nasty Mortgage

Most people think that there are no tricks to getting rid of their mortgage. The truth is that there really is a bit of "magic" — the astonishing effect that prepayments and increased frequency payments can have on the life of your after-tax debt. In other words, while it is clearly not rocket science that if you pay more money, or pay more frequently, you will owe less, what is surprising is how much you can save. Another revelation is just how easy it is for you to figure out what the potential savings can be due to any change in your payment habits.

Any extra payments made at the beginning of the life cycle of the mortgage yield exponential benefits. Every $100 extra that you pay at the beginning saves you over $400 over the term (based on average interest rates). That's an incredible return.

The following are the key ways to reduce your mortgage.

1. Increase the amount you pay. You can increase the amount once per year or each period you make payments. The idea here is to add an extra $50 or $100 to your payment or to accumulate a sum and pay it annually and watch the savings grow. The way this works is simple: the more you prepay, the less there is for the lender to charge you interest on. If the principal is lower and you maintain the same level of payments, then more of what you pay goes towards further principal reduction rather than to interest. Most mortgages have an allowance for an annual sum that you can pay down your principal with. Ordinarily, that number is between 10% and 15% of the mortgage — even for what is labelled a closed mortgage! For example, if you have a $100,000 mortgage at 7% for five years, with a 25-year amortization (all very average numbers), you would be paying $700.42 per month. It would take 25 years to fully pay off the mortgage (the amortization). If you paid an extra $1,000 in the first year in a lump sum, you would end up saving $4,122.45 in interest over the life of the mortgage. Your amortization would also go down — by a full seven months! If you increased your payment on the same mortgage by an extra 10% per month, the net result would be a savings of over $23,000 and a reduction in your amortization by four years and nine months! Not only can you save a pile of money, but you also shorten the life of your mortgage. Consider calculating the net benefit of the prepayment and compare that to the return you might expect from other sorts of fixed return investments. An average prepayment, when viewed in comparison to other fixed return investments (in terms of return on investment), yields a return of about 11% before tax. Compare that to what a GIC would pay you at your local bank. Of course, you could always merely opt for a shorter amortization term, thereby increasing your payments. This is great if you can afford to make higher payments, because the interest savings over the life of the mortgage can be significant. For example, a $100,000 mortgage at 8% that has its amortization period reduced from 25 years to 15 years would result in interest savings of over $50,000!

2.   Pay more often. Many mortgages allow you to pay biweekly instead of monthly. Think about this! Ordinarily, you make 12 equal mortgage payments per year. Because a biweekly payment scheme means 26 payments (52 divided by two) you essentially end up making the equivalent of one extra monthly mortgage payment per year. That payment goes straight towards the bottom-line principal and will save you thousands of dollars over the course of the lifetime of an average mortgage. The amount you save relates directly to your interest rate and when you start making the bi-weekly payments. Use the following example as a guide. Suppose you have a $100,000 mortgage for a 5-year term at 7% interest with a typical 25-year amortization. If you made the monthly payments of $700.42, after 5 years, you would still owe $91,044.30. But, if you were to pay biweekly ($350.21 every two weeks instead of $700.42 every month), at the end of the 5 years you would owe $86,792.54! The five extra payments totalling $3,502.10 saves you $4,251.76 in the end sum owing. These calculations are easy to do on the Internet. A good site is **www.gemortgage.ca**, which has a "prepayment analyzer" feature.

3.   Take advantage of "double up" privileges. Many mortgages contain a feature that allows you to double a payment and then skip the same number of payments that you have doubled. This feature was originally designed to help people with inconsistent cash flow, such as those who are self-employed or who work on a seasonal or commission basis. The idea is that you pay more when you have the money and skip payments when you do not. However, others can avail themselves of this feature and use it to pay more down on their principal. Remember: the more you lower your principal, the less there is for the lender to charge interest on — which translates into big savings.

4.   Get the maximum RRSP rebate and use it towards principal reduction. Surprisingly, many people do not take advantage of the ability to borrow for an RRSP. Consider borrowing to obtain the maximum

RRSP you can and then use the tax savings to pay down the principal. Doing that will result in a savings that lasts the life of the mortgage. Similarly, any windfall monies, like inheritances, that are applied to the mortgage will reap big dividends in interest savings.

As with about everything in life, there is a bit more to all this. For example, putting all your money into the mortgage, while being fiscally prudent, reduces your liquidity. It's nice to be able to write a cheque for something when you need to. Some homeowners arrange a line of credit against their house for this very reason — only paying interest on what they actually use. This makes much sense, and as a result products like this are very popular. Others avail themselves of newer products like the "Manulife One," which combines all their business (mortgage, chequing, and savings) into one account, and saves interest costs as a result, while maintaining liquidity. Products such as this are all the rage in Europe — expect to see more in Canada soon.

Sometimes, it does not make sense to put extra money into the mortgage. If, for example, you have credit card debt at 19%, it makes better sense to pay that off before working on the mortgage, which may be in the range of 7%.

You need to calculate the net effect of the prepayment or enlarged payment and compare it with the return on other investments or against the true cost of your other debts to determine if prepayment makes sense for you. The Internet is full of great calculators that help in figuring all this out (see Appendix 1). Most bank Web sites have them — especially good are the ones at **www.cimbl.ca** and at **www.gemortgage.ca**, or you can ask your financial adviser for assistance.

How To Make Your Mortgage Tax Deductible

Residential mortgages are generally not tax deductible; however, there is a way to make the mortgage deductible that generally works in certain circumstances. The idea is that if you borrow money to make money, then the interest on your borrowed money is tax deductible.

According to the federal government: "You can claim the following carrying charges and interest you paid to earn income from investments: most interest you pay on money you borrow, but generally only as long as you use it to earn investment income, including interest and dividends. However, if the only earnings your investment can produce are capital gains, you cannot claim the interest you paid."[7]

There is a bit of a debate as to whether stocks or mutual funds qualify, but the general consensus is that they do — and homeowners are well advised to consult with their accountant or tax lawyer to verify this.

To make your mortgage essentially tax deductible involves an exchange of assets. Simply put, sell your investment assets and convert them to cash. Pay whatever tax is generated (there may be a capital gain or a capital loss) and use the available cash to either reduce the amount you owe on your mortgage or pay it off completely. Then, arrange a replacement or fresh mortgage and use that money to buy back the investments you previously held — or perhaps some new ones.

With this mechanism, you end up still having a mortgage on your house and still owning the investments. The difference, though, is that you have borrowed money to earn investment income, making the interest you pay deductible. There are things to be aware of, such as the aforementioned capital gains, as well as prepayment penalties that may exist on your mortgage. Check into those issues first. You may have an open mortgage that allows you to pay down without penalty, or it may be that you are using this mechanism when your closed mortgage matures, meaning no penalties can apply.

If your house has no mortgage, this is even simpler. You can use your house as security in order to manouevre your assets to take advantage of this tax deduction as just about every lender has secured lines of credit products available at historically low interest rates. Because your real estate asset secures the loan, you qualify for essentially bargain interest rates. You simply borrow from the house equity, buy the right investments and the interest you pay is deductible.

Tracking Interest Rates

It's an everyday ritual. The prospective homebuyer or borrower runs each day to the business section of the local paper, trying to obtain a sense of where interest rates are going. The direction can be significant and can impact buying decisions. The reality is that if you want to guess whether interest rates are increasing or decreasing, you'd better first have a look at the bond market. The state of the economy affects bond rates, and what happens in the bond market translates directly to what Canadians pay for their mortgages.

The way this works is as follows. Governments (and some corporations), like everyone, need money. They have a seemingly never-ending need to raise money to pay for their various initiatives. They do this in part by issuing bonds. A bond is really nothing more than a promise to pay, along with scheduled interest. It is an instrument used to raise funds, acting basically as a loan to the issuer from the buyer. How long the bond is out for and the rate of interest paid on the bond varies, in some measure due to the prevailing government economic strategy.

The total of all the bonds issued and outstanding by the government is called the national debt. The bonds are usually sold to institutional investors, such as pension funds, which then view them as a sort of commodity, namely something that can be resold to others.

Bonds fluctuate in value generally due to three basic reasons, namely, "the outlook for inflation, the outlook for the Canadian dollar, and the riskiness of the bond."[8] For example, if something bad happens with the economy or there is a political issue, investors may become wary of putting money into Canada (buying Canadian bonds), with the result that the value of the bond will fall. And when the value of the bond falls, the interest rate is effectively increased.

The result is that banks tend to watch what goes on in the bond market carefully, so that they can adjust their loan and deposit rates as they need to. Simply put, the bond market shows banks what the market price is for money at any given time. And if the banks do not lend a homebuyer $200,000 to buy a house (which earns them for example, $14,000 per year less what they pay their depositors) they could, in theory, simply buy a bond and earn $11,000. The extra $3,000 they get from the homebuyer covers their costs of dealing with the homebuyer and represents a "retail margin." Banks owe a duty to shareholders and depositors to use the money left with them on deposit in the "best" way. They can put the money out in commercial lending, or they can invest in bonds (rate determinable) or they can lend it out to homebuyers. The idea for them is to get enough of a premium from homebuyers (or owners financing existing houses) over what they can earn from bonds or from commercial lending to cover the increased costs and risks involved in lending at the retail level. Those costs include mortgage broker fees, branches, staff, and much more. Generally, the premium as described is about 2% to 2.7% but it does vary and fluctuate.

What goes on in the bond market directly affects what goes on in the mortgage market — insofar as rates are established. The market for bonds tends to go up when the stock market goes down. When the stock market is declining, many investors choose to put their money into bonds — where they earn interest — rather than stocks, where the principal of the investment may be eroded. When the demand for bonds increases (such as when there is bad economic news that drives investors from the stock market to the more certain bond market), so do bond prices. Higher bond prices mean lower bond yields (return on investment). When the yield on bonds declines, generally, so do mortgage rates. Of course, the same scenario can play out in reverse.

What does all this mean to the average mortgage borrower? According to economist Peter Norman of Clayton Research, "the retail lending rates that homeowners face when financing a purchase or renovation are directly affected by activity in the bond market, which itself is affected by investors' confidence in Canadian institutions and companies, and the outlook for inflation and exchange rates in Canada."[9]

Mortgage rates are subject to the whims of the economy. To predict where interest rates are going means predicting investor confidence in our economy, as well as inflation and our exchange rate. That's a tricky thing to do. But keeping an eye on the bond market, which is what the banks are doing, will at least give you an idea of what is going on today, which may help in figuring out what will go on tomorrow.

Things To Keep in Mind

In taking out a mortgage, you are likely borrowing more than you will for any other thing in your personal life. Pitfalls abound. The way you shop, the type of mortgage you choose, and how you repay it all have strong implications for your overall financial health. There are things you can do to make all of this better for you financially.

- Understand the different types of mortgages and be ready to discuss them with prospective lenders.

- Get a copy of your credit report and ensure there are no mistakes; if you have no credit history, get one: borrow for an RRSP or get a credit card and make timely payments, as lenders may reject your application if they can't see your credit history.

- Consider getting a mortgage pre-approval, which lets you know exactly how much you have to play with, as well as protects you against rate increases for 60 days, but does not obligate you to deal with the lender that gave you the pre-approval.

- Decide whether to go to a bank or other lenders directly or use a mortgage broker.

- Don't damage your credit rating just before shopping for a mortgage.

- Don't buy a car while shopping for a mortgage or just after being approved.

- Don't quit or change jobs.

- Get professional advice.

- Consider a second mortgage in order to avoid paying default insurance if you have the ability to pay down a mortgage quickly.

- If you have to join the sub-prime market in order to get a loan, don't lock yourself in for a long time.

- Look at the spread between long- and short-term rates to help you decide whether to lock in to a long-term mortgage or a short-term one.

- If you are renewing your mortgage, consider shopping around and negotiating with different lenders in order to get the best deal, rather than simply remaining with your current lender.

- In order to reduce your mortgage, consider: increasing the amount you pay, paying more often; taking advantage of "doubling up" privileges; and using the maximum RRSP rebate to reduce your principal.

- Think about making your mortgage tax deductible by manouevring your investment assets to make the interest you pay tax deductible.

- And, lastly, look to the bond market as an indicator as to where interest rates are headed.

Almost everyone who buys a house gets some kind of mortgage. Regardless of which mortgage you choose, entering the world of home ownership is an exciting and financially rewarding experience. Often times, a level of risk has to be assumed in order to profit, and in that respect, making money from home ownership is not different than many other "for profit" ventures. Most people have to borrow to make it happen.

As with so many things in life, it's best to educate yourself on the various nuances of the many products out there in order to maximize the financial benefits of house ownership. Understanding the options and using that understanding to select the product that best matches your financial situation can only help your financial health.

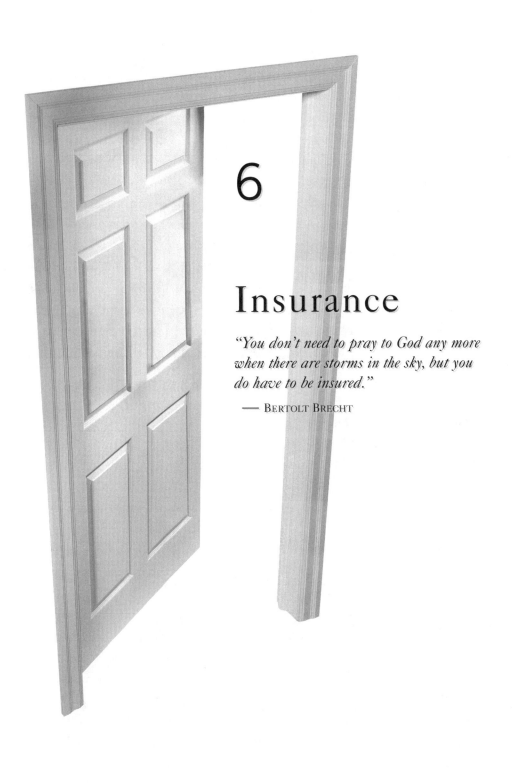

6

Insurance

"You don't need to pray to God any more when there are storms in the sky, but you do have to be insured."

— BERTOLT BRECHT

Can peace of mind and home ownership coexist? Insurance people sure think so. They offer a number of insurance products to homeowners in order to provide them with some protection and peace of mind regarding their largest and most prized investment. Like anything, there is a price attached; peace of mind is not cheap. Understanding the options when it comes to the world of insurance will help you select what is best for you based on your circumstances.

This chapter reviews the most important types of insurance that you need to consider buying, without any sales hype. The focus here is a bit different than elsewhere in this book. Rather than provide you with advice on how to proactively get the most financially out of your exercise in home ownership, this chapter focuses on the issue of how to protect what is yours. Prudent homeowners interested in protecting their investment should pay extra attention to this chapter. The right kind of insurance can, in some circumstances, make the difference between financial devastation and financial salvation.

Mortgage Life Insurance

Face it, no one lives forever and no one can plan their death so that it occurs at a time convenient to their financial planning. What if you die and there is still money owing on your mortgage? Who will pay it? Where will the money come from? How will the first payment on the mortgage after you die be made? Do you want your family to have to deal with a financial crisis when you die? Since the mortgage on your house is the largest debt you are likely to incur in your lifetime, it makes sense to consider the issue of life insurance in the context of home ownership.

Although you may hear of mortgage life insurance being called simply "mortgage insurance," that is really a misnomer. In the true sense, "mortgage insurance" refers to insurance the lender gets against your defaulting on your payments, the cost of which is typically paid by the borrower. But that sort of insurance is usually called "default insurance," and in Canada is readily available from GE Capital and CMHC on high-ratio mortgages (where the borrower is borrowing more than 75% of the value of the house).

Mortgage life insurance is a form of life insurance that pays off your mortgage when you die. Typically, you buy mortgage life insurance from the lender that funds your mortgage, and it is often less expensive than buying directly from a private life insurance company (although that savings comes at a price, namely some restrictions). Generally, the monthly payment for municipal property taxes is also included in the benefit and it can also include total disability coverage. The amount of coverage decreases as your mortgage balance declines.

There is no law, of course, that says you must have any form of life insurance, but it does make good financial sense to consider. The general rule is that if you have children or other dependents who would suffer financially should you die, then you would be well advised to have some form of life insurance. If you do choose to get life insurance, you have a couple of options: you can buy insurance from the bank or lender that gave you your mortgage or you can buy it from a life insurance company.

The essential difference between the two primary options is that if you buy mortgage life insurance from the bank or lender, and you die while there is still money owing on the mortgage, the policy pays off the outstanding balance directly to the bank. On the other hand, if you buy a policy from an insurance company, when you die, the proceeds of the policy go directly to your beneficiaries.

If you are a young family that is cash-strapped, buying mortgage life insurance directly from a bank can result in big savings. It generally costs less to buy mortgage life insurance from a bank than it does to buy life insurance from an insurance company. You don't have to deal with insurance sales people and the savings of not having that middleman advise you may be one of the reasons for the general cost savings. Also, the bank's products typically do not involve any investment component, which is another reason for the lower price.

One benefit of buying from the bank is that the bank arranges everything for you, and the money you pay can come out with your mortgage payment. The amount of coverage you get matches your need — if your need is to have the house debt cleared on death.

The downside of buying from a bank is that you might sell the house or switch banks. If that happens, you have to apply again for mortgage life insurance. Being approved is not automatic, but subject to health qualifications. If you have health problems at that time, you may not qualify. The benefit is also paid to the bank, which uses it to pay off the regular balance owing on the mortgage. It does not go directly to your beneficiaries, who then can't make the decision themselves if they would rather the money go elsewhere. (They might want to do this if you had a great mortgage rate that they wanted to keep.)

Life Insurance

The other alternative to buying mortgage life insurance from a bank, as we saw, is buying life insurance from an insurance company, which, upon your death, pays out an amount of money to your beneficiaries directly. Some people prefer the freedom and flexibility offered by life insurance products, since they allow your beneficiaries to decide where the money will go — either paying down the mortgage or maintaining the mortgage (if they have a good rate) and investing it elsewhere. There is no definitive answer as to which option is best; it really is a matter of which option better suits your individual needs.

Generally, people buy enough insurance to pay for what they believe their family will need if they die to cover things such as funeral costs, ongoing groceries, and living expenses, including the mortgage and other loans as well as children's education costs.

Like many issues relating to the world of insurance, options abound. While there are numerous life insurance products, all of them fall into two basic types of policies: term insurance and permanent insurance.

Term Life Insurance

Term life insurance is insurance for a specified period of time. Ordinarily, people choose a term of 5 or 10 years, although you can buy terms ranging from 1 to 25 years. When the term expires, it's up to you to renew — and the renewal is ordinarily at a higher premium, because you are then that much older. Once you reach 65 to 70 years old, you cannot buy term insurance. Generally, term insurance is the most affordable type. If you die within the term, the policy is paid out to your beneficiary.

There are two basic types of term policies: "level term" and "decreasing or declining term." A level term policy means that the premium you pay and the benefit on death are fixed for the duration of the term. It is considered a good starter's policy because it is generally less expensive than permanent insurance, and you can arrange enough coverage to meet your protection needs for a fixed time. For example, if you only feel that you need coverage until your children enter the workforce, you can arrange a term policy that lasts that long. Once they are out of the house and working, your protection needs may drop and you can then not renew or renew for a different amount and term.

Some Canadian insurers offer "term to 100" policies that pay a benefit if you die before the age of 100 and allow for the premium to remain constant regardless of your age or health.

A decreasing or declining term policy features a benefit that declines at a fixed rate over the term. Generally, people select this to match what they owe on a mortgage. The idea is to have enough protection to pay off the mortgage during the term. As the mortgage debt declines, so does your coverage and, with that, the cost.

Permanent Insurance

Permanent insurance is generally more complex than term coverage. The biggest difference is the savings element of the policy. In other words, a value is created that is much like a savings account — although getting at the money while you are alive varies among the different types of policies.

With permanent insurance, the coverage is for life and has no limitation based on term: it's good until you die. The premiums are generally set for life and cannot be changed, regardless of what happens to your health subsequent to the acceptance of the policy. At the beginning of the policy life, the premium is higher than it would be for a term policy generally, because the policyholder is younger. The idea is to build up a reserve to level out the increased risk in future years. That reserve is held in cash and becomes the cash value of the policy. It is possible that the reserve will pay for the entirety of the policy at some point, making the policy "paid up." The use of the reserve varies depending on the type of policy.

With permanent policies, described as "whole life," the premiums are fixed so long as the policy is in effect. As you continue to pay premiums, a cash value is created. That cash value is paid out in the form of dividends — which can then effectively be used to lower the premiums paid or buy more insurance.

A permanent variable life insurance policy provides that a portion of what you pay as premium goes into what is called a "cash value account." That money is then invested in different types of securities. When you die, the benefit is made up of two parts, namely the guaranteed part (backed by the insurer) and the variable part, which is what your cash value account is worth. That amount can vary, depending on how well the investments have performed. You are allowed to borrow from the policy, but you are not able to withdraw money during your lifetime. You are also not able to change the policy amount or the amount of protection.

A permanent universal life policy (it has an insurance and a savings portion) provides more control than the variable or whole life. You can borrow against the value of the policy or withdraw money from it. You can maintain the premiums for life or you can pay off the policy, should you so desire. You also have flexibility in the amount of coverage you acquire.

Both term and permanent life insurance have features that are attractive to many people. Generally, term insurance is less expensive; making it the insurance of choice for cash-strapped young families. The downside, of course, is that when you try to renew after the term expires, you may have to requalify (meaning a new health test) and, because you are older, the policy price goes up. Term insurance carries no cash value. Permanent insurance, while generally more expensive, does not have increasing premiums — they stay level. People who sell permanent insurance will tell you that their policies have a cash savings value, which is true, but the cash may not necessarily be a good deal. Many argue that you are far better off financially by taking the savings (from buying term versus permanent) and investing that money yourself. Investing it yourself offers you the flexibility of selecting exactly where your money is going. If you are lucky and invest well, you may be far ahead of the game than if you had left your cash value to the insurance fund managers. Consider also that once you reach 65 or 70, you may not even have an option because no one will sell you term policies at that age. There really is no hard and fast rule as to which policy is better — it all depends on your individual needs.

As with so many things in life, when it comes to this very important issue, it pays to shop around. The range in pricing between bank insurance and private insurance can be significant, with banks often (but not always) having the lower price. It is probably best to shoot for the best of both worlds, namely have some insurance on the mortgage from the bank, as well as having a separate policy from a private insurer so as to allow your family some choice (they may need money for living expenses) upon your death. Consulting a reputable insurance broker or your financial planner will help you decide what is best for you.

Whichever route you choose, always remember that with your significant real estate investment comes responsibility to those who depend on you. For many, home ownership is not only the cornerstone of retirement planning, but also an essential part of what they leave behind. Taking appropriate steps to ensure that you don't leave your family with a financial disaster just makes so much sense.

Fire Insurance

If you are financing your home purchase by means of a mortgage, you will have to arrange for fire insurance to cover the property *from the day of closing*. You can arrange this through an insurance broker, who should be able to tailor a policy to suit your needs. Buying an insurance policy and selecting a broker is not like buying a commodity; price should be a factor, but not the determining one. A good broker will provide you with good service, whether that is in the form of updating you on new products or being there to help you when there is a claim. The broker should advise you on what coverage you really need so as to get you the best price. Sometimes, it helps to ask if there are discounts offered by a particular insurance company for having more than one policy with them. If you place your life and auto policy with one company, you may get a better deal. Ask whether or not the insurance company offers discounts for having smoke detectors, dead bolt locks, fire extinguishers, and alarm systems in the home.

Some brokers will shop multiple inusurers on your behalf, and other brokers work exclusively with one company. Either way, you should advise your insurance broker of the name, address, phone, and fax number of both your lawyer and of the lender providing your mortgage. The lender must be noted on the policy, and your lawyer requires a letter (known as a "binder letter") confirming that insurance coverage is in place effective on closing and noting the interest of the lender in the property. Be sure to explain the importance of this to your insurance broker, as the lender will not advance funds to close your purchase until they know that there is insurance on the property. Failure of the insurance broker to deliver the binder letter is one of the most common causes of delayed closings (and grey hair for the lawyer!).

Lenders insist on a policy of fire insurance that notes their interest in the property on closing before they advance funds because they need to be assured that their mortgage will get paid even if your house burns down. By naming them as insured, and by ensuring you have enough coverage to replace the building, the lender's loan is protected.

Shopping for home fire insurance can be confusing. The following is an outline of what you need to know.

Replacement Cost

This endorsement deals with the contents of the house. It means that if you suffer a loss to your personal property (damaged or stolen) either on or off the property where the home is located, you are entitled to compensation for the full replacement value as opposed to the lower actual or depreciated value.

Replacement Guarantee

This endorsement ensures that in the event of a total loss (for example if the house burns down to the ground), the dwelling will be replaced exactly as it was before the loss, regardless of the cost of reconstruction. The insurance broker will ask you questions relating to the size of the home, number of bathrooms, fireplaces, and other features of the home in order to arrive at a figure for what they call "appropriate coverage," which they use to base the premium on. Remember that this figure reflects their opinion of what they think it will cost to rebuild the home if there is a total loss. The figure will be less than the purchase price because the purchase price reflects the value of both the land and the home and there is no need to insure the land. Further, market conditions may affect the purchase price but may not necessarily affect the replacement cost of the actual home.

Third-Party Liability Coverage

This endorsement protects you (and members of your family who also live in the house) against claims made by others (not members of the same household) in certain circumstances. These types of claims typically relate to things like an injury to someone who slips and falls while on your property, as well as damage that you cause inadvertently to someone else's property.

Basic Perils

Most policies will also cover you for basic perils such as fire, theft, windstorm, vandalism, and burglary. Many homeowners "top up" their coverage with "extras" such as coverage for sewer backup, computers, and home business coverage.

Named Peril or All Risk?

The named peril policy will insure only for the perils named specifically in the policy, whereas an all risk policy will cover all risks, except those specifically excluded. An all risk policy will typically (but not necessarily) cover more than a named peril policy. No policy covers everything!

Title Insurance

It has always surprised me that so many people go into the whole business of buying a home trusting all along the way. Any seasoned real estate lawyer will tell you that it is almost impossible to predict the kind of things that can go wrong. Moreover, it is impossible to protect yourself against absolutely every event. Lawyer due diligence can only do so much. Unknown defects and issues can arise that harm you financially, the best efforts of the best lawyer notwithstanding. Title insurance is not a cure-all, but it clearly is better than the old process of only relying on the lawyer's opinion on title to cover all aspects of your claim to title on a house. Some title problems that are covered by title insurance policies can be scary indeed. In many instances, an unprotected closing can result in a financial devastation, such as being the victim of some frauds and forgeries.

The use of title insurance in Canada by lawyers has grown by leaps and bounds in recent years. Yet, despite the fact that it has become a mainstream product, its benefits are relatively unknown to consumers. Canadians are very aware of the benefits of other forms of insurance — we insure our lives, our cars, and the building we live in. But what about the quality of our title? How can we be sure we have acquired the bundle of rights to the property that we think we have? Are there unknown problems lurking within? What about protection against risks that threaten our right to enjoy the title to our homes? After all, we spend more on our homes than on any other single item we own.

What Is Title Insurance?

Title insurance is a one-time policy issued at the time of the closing of a real estate transaction, which lasts as long as you own the property. It provides protection to the buyer or lender, or both against a variety of perils that relate to the quality of title acquired by the buyer and the security against the house that the lender has. Simply put, it is an assurance of the bundle of rights acquired by the buyer, lender, or both on closing. When buying a house, it can only be obtained through your lawyer.

What makes title insurance so essential is not only the hitherto unavailable level of protection, but also the efficiencies lawyers are able to enjoy when they process your purchase using a title insurance policy. It used to be (in what I call the "old world") that the lawyer, in closing a purchase, had to do two types of searches: title and off title. In a title search, the lawyer looks back in time to verify that the seller acquired title correctly and has the ability in law to deliver to you what is known as clear title. Off title searches are mostly municipal and provincial government searches that address issues such as whether the property complies with all the appropriate bylaws and more. Further, the lawyer checks that there are no arrears of things that can impact on the clarity of title — such as property tax arrears. That kind of debt runs with the property, and one of the lawyer's responsibilities is to verify if there are arrears, and, if so, to adjust what is owing up to the day of closing. At the end of the day, the lawyer provides something called an "opinion" on title. The opinion is just that — a collection of the lawyer's thoughts on the quality of title based on the results of the searches performed.

In a closing where the lawyer is using title insurance, the deal closes not based on what the lawyer's opinion is as to the quality of title you are acquiring, but on the strength of the policy of insurance that the lawyer arranges for you and the lender. The policy provides assurance to the buyer and the lender as to the bundle of rights each acquires to the title of the property. The lawyer still does searches (and in fact has to report the search results to the insurer), but the introduction of a risk taker (the insurer) into a process where conventionally no one assumed any risk allows for a better, faster, and cheaper closing.

The assurance offered by a title insurer is backed by deep-pocket American insurance companies. There are several title insurance companies operating in Canada, and they all involve U.S. firms, either as direct insurers or insurers covering the title portion of the risk. That's a good thing for Canadian consumers, who benefit not only from the century of experience the U.S. insurers have in assuring title, but also from the financial strength these large firms bring to the real estate marketplace. This financial strength is typically greater than any of the lawyer's malpractice insurers.

Benefits of Title Insurance

Quite simply, a title insured closing provides greater protection for the consumer and lender than an uninsured closing. But the benefits are far more than that. They include a smoother process and a greater likelihood that your deal will close on time and uneventfully.

It's a direct insured no fault claims process.
In an "old world" closing, if the lawyer did all the searches he or she was supposed to and exercised ordinary due diligence in the work performed, and something turned out to be wrong, rendering the opinion wrong, the lawyer would ordinarily not be responsible. For the lawyer to be responsible, generally, the standard of care he or she exercised in the conveyance process has to be deficient somehow. The difficulty in all this, from a consumer perspective, is that the "insured" is not the consumer or the lender, but rather the lawyer. To access the insurance, the victim (consumer or lender) is up against the lawyer's professional liability insurer; the victim must be able to demonstrate that the lawyer did something wrong in the conveyance. That can be difficult, as standards of

conveyance work change from time to time and from community to community. If the insurer disputes the claim and you are forced to go to court to obtain compensation, you then are into the world of costly litigation. I use "costly" in the kindest sense here — truthfully, the cost of a lawsuit these days is beyond ridiculous.

When your lawyer places title insurance on your property in processing your deal, you and your lender become the direct insured. A title insurance claim is a no fault claim, and you are directly insured. The process of collecting on a claim often starts with a mere phone call. That process is far superior to the old process of going after the lawyer first.

Consider this. Just about every bank in Canada has a program with one of the title insurers operating in Canada whereby they process their non-purchase transactions (such as refinance or secured lines of credit) in conjunction with a title insurance policy. You really have to wonder whether the banks know something that ordinary consumers don't. The answer is that they do. The banks are the ones, for years, who put their money out, in part on the strength of lawyer's opinion on title. When there was a problem, they were the ones who had to bear it. Title insurance changes that; it leaves them the direct insured and has a no fault claims process. The banks figured out long ago that they are better off with a title insurance policy than without. There is a compelling lesson for consumers here!

Title insurance saves you money.

In the past several years, governments (both municipal and provincial) have looked to title and off title searches as revenue generators and have steadily increased the cost they charge to lawyers for the search results. At the same time, the time to respond to search requests has often also been extended — slowing down many closings. To make matters worse, these searches often reveal little information and are usually marked "E & OE": errors and omissions excepted! In my mind they should really state, "WCSUATINY-CDAI" short for, "We Can Screw Up and There is Nothing You Can Do About It."

In a title insured transaction, the policy acts as a risk taker, assuming reasonable risk in exchange for a premium. When the lawyer uses title insurance, the need for certain searches becomes unnecessary as the results of those searches are covered by the policy. The money saved by not doing these searches can, in some cases, be greater than the cost of the policy. The savings vary within Canada, but generally is greatest in Ontario and the Maritimes, and less in the prairie provinces and B.C. Moreover, you avoid the whole "E & OE" nonsense because you obtain direct coverage.

Title insurance eliminates the lender's requirement for a survey.

Across Canada, just about every lender requires a buyer to produce an up-to-date survey in order to obtain the mortgage funds. The lender needs the survey to be sure that the house has not been built in such a way so as to obstruct things like easements or conflict with municipal setback requirements (how far away the house or deck should be from the lot line). This is a simple requirement. But what often happens is that the survey is old and does not show things such as alterations or additions or decks. Sometimes, a very old existing survey has simply been photocopied too many times and is hence not clear. When that happens (think "old world"), a new survey has to be obtained. The cost of a new survey ranges in Canada from about $150 in the western part of the country to about $800 in Ontario. Moreover, problems with existing surveys often appear at the very last minute, since that's when lenders tend to look at them — just before a scheduled closing. The closing then has to be delayed to obtain the new survey.

Just about all mortgage companies and banks (certainly any major ones) will accept a policy of title insurance in lieu of a survey. Since the cost of the survey is greater than the cost of the title insurance policy most of the time, that translates into savings for consumers. That savings become even greater when compounded with the effect of avoiding the cost of unnecessary searches.

Title insurance provides broader protection than the lawyer's opinion on title.

Without sounding too alarmist, there are risks out there that could imperil the quality of your investment in your house; a lawyer, doing an "old world" closing, cannot protect you against these risks and title insurance can. The most obvious of those risks are fraud and forgeries relating to your title, such as someone else claiming to own an interest in your title or claiming to have a lien against your house. These types of problems tend to be catastrophic in nature — and the best way to avoid these nightmare scenarios is to have title insurance. Other covered matters include documents in the chain of title not being validly registered; liens on the property (such as for nonpayment of taxes); certain work orders; and forced removal of structures (except for boundary walls and fences) because they violate zoning bylaws or they extend onto adjoining properties. Many other items, such as special assessments for improvements, and a variety of title defects are also covered.

Talk Is Cheap — The Proof Is In the Pudding

Fraud and forgery with regard to home ownership is a bigger problem than most care to admit. The thing about fraud and forgeries is that the victims (most of the time, there seems to be a mortgage involved) tend not to want to talk about it. The last thing any bank wants to publicize is that they were stung by a fraud. Yet the problem is so big that CMHC recently hosted a series of seminars across Canada with industry leaders such as First Canadian Title and the RCMP to raise awareness of fraud in the lending and real estate industry. In Ontario, the lawyers' malpractice insurer recently distributed special literature to lawyers offering advice on avoiding being drawn into frauds.

There are many examples of fraud and forgery when it comes to real estate deals. How do you know the seller is really who they say they are? Do you think the listing agent asked for photo identification when they took the listing? Stories abound of tenants impersonating owners, girlfriends impersonating wives, and more. If you buy a property in a circumstance such as described in this section, you may be buying something from someone who did not have authority to sell it — because it is not theirs! You could be a victim of a fraud!

There is no better way to portray why I feel every homebuyer should have a title policy on their home than to portray actual examples of what has happened to real Canadians. The following stories are all true. (The claims stories are all courtesy of First Canadian Title.)

The Phony Baloney Tenant

In a recent incident in B.C., a landlord who lived offshore rented a house to a tenant in Victoria. The tenant impersonated the true owner and listed and sold the house to an unsuspecting buyer. The buyer's lawyers did all the right searches and everything seemed to be in order. The new owners took possession and began renovating the house. One day, a man came up to them at the house and said something along the lines of, "What have you done to my house?" Can you imagine someone saying that to you? The new buyers are now facing a financial disaster, although they are the innocent victims of fraud (since the tenant did not own the property, he had no legal authority to sell. In law, you can't sell what is not yours). Had their lawyer title insured their purchase, they would have been protected, since the policy covers fraud and forgeries in the circumstances described. Their case has yet to be settled, but it serves as a good warning story of the unknown perils buyers face.

The Fraudulently Discharged Mortgage

Mr. X owned a home in Ontario. One day he decided to perpetrate a fraud. He went to a local stationer and bought a mortgage discharge form, which is a form of public notice that the mortgage is no longer a charge on title once it is registered. (This is the form the Registry Office accepts when a mortgage is paid off.) Mr. X filled out the form with the name of the lender and forged the signature of a signing official. He then took the forged form to the local Registry Office, paid the registration fee to the registrar, and registered the discharge onto his title. This is an ordinary everyday type of registration. The effect of it is that it shows that the charge the lender registered is no longer valid.

Our errant villain then proceeded to list and sell the house. Mr. and Mrs. Y bought it. They hired a lawyer, who used the "old world" system. The lawyer searched title and proceeded in the ordinary course. The search of title revealed that the old mortgage had been discharged, so the lawyer acting for Mr. and Mrs. Y did not ask the seller's (Mr. X's) lawyer for a discharge — it was already done. On closing, the buyers paid the seller's lawyer the proceeds of the purchase. The seller's lawyer would ordinarily pay off whatever mortgages were shown outstanding, but, in this case, there was nothing registered as outstanding, so the seller's lawyer paid the entire proceed of the sale over to the seller, Mr. X.

A short while after closing, someone came to the door of the home of Mr. and Mrs. Y. When they answered the door, they were met with a stranger, who looked at them and said, "Who are you and what are you doing here in this house?" They responded by indicating that they owned the house and produced their deed. The stranger was a representative of the lender who held the mortgage that Mr. X had fraudulently discharged.

Mr. and Mrs. Y pointed their fingers at their own lawyer, saying that she must have done something wrong. She responded, correctly, by stating that she did all the searches she was required to do. They then looked to the seller's lawyer, who similarly responded by saying that everything was done correctly (which it was). After all, the buyer's lawyer had done what they were supposed to do (the search) and it revealed no mortgage outstanding. The seller's lawyer, similarly, had no reason not to pay the closing proceeds to the seller.

The lender in all this was clearly not impressed and sued, forcing Mr. and Mrs. Y to learn a painful and expensive lesson about the Canadian legal system.

The battle was one of priorities — whose interest was paramount? Would it be that of the innocent family or that of the lender who had the mortgage on title that Mr. X had fraudulently discharged?

In the end, after several years of this family defending the title to the property they had bought, the court ordered the province's assurance fund to pay out the lender because they had registered a phony document. That's great for the lender, but the family had legal bills in excess of $30,000!!! (I might have suggested earlier that lawyers don't come cheap.) That money was spent defending the title that their lawyer told them was clearly theirs. After some prodding the provincial government fund coughed up the legal fees and paid that, too.

There are many things that are disturbing in this story. One of them is that the family had to spend their first few years of home ownership worrying about whether they could keep the home they paid for. That must have been a nightmare for them. Another disturbing feature of this story is that the lawyers involved did absolutely nothing wrong and could not have prevented this disaster from happening.

Fortunately, there is a simple way to avoid that nightmare — be sure your lawyer title insures your property. All title insurers in Canada offer coverage for fraud and forgery relating to title.

The Encroaching Bathtub

A first-time home buyer purchased a 90-year-old row house in a modest section of a mid-sized Ontario city. Shortly after moving in, the next-door neighbour advised that when the second floor was added to the buyer's home many years before, the previous owners built over the party wall. The buyer's bathtub was actually sitting over the party wall and encroached onto his property. Can you imagine that? The neighbour figured all this out when he saw water damage in his ceiling and opened the ceiling only to find the pipes from the first-time buyer's bathtub on his side of the line. When confronted, the previous owners claimed that they had forgotten about it and didn't think it was important to mention. So much for sellers' integrity! The realtor had no knowledge of the problem. A survey would not likely have revealed the discrepancy.

The title insurer reviewed the policy and was able to find coverage under the policy. Technically, the bathtub encroached over the property line. Renovations, which consisted of gutting much of the second floor of the home, were done at the insurer's expense at a time convenient to the buyer. The buyer was given accommodation in a hotel for the two weeks it took to complete the renovations. She was also compensated for the fact that her home was 20 square feet smaller than she thought it was.

Encroachment Issues

An encroachment means that a part of a structure or fence is not where it is supposed to be. Typically, encroachments happen by accident and are usually done unwittingly. They tend to involve things like eaves from the roof or a deck that is too close to the setback from the neighbour's property line required by a local bylaw. Sometimes, a structure can be built right over the property line and actually be built all or partially onto a neighbour's property. The fact that a house has been there for a long time does not minimize the chances of this sort of problem happening. Title insurance provides protection in many cases from losses due to encroachments when no survey is obtained.

In one recent case, a couple purchased a property. They ordered that a new survey be done; however, just before closing, the surveyor told them that the survey would not be completed prior to closing. They purchased title insurance. After closing, they received the up-to-date survey, and it showed minor encroachments of the eaves onto an adjoining property, the encroachment of the walkway and driveway onto city property, and the encroachment of some steps onto a rear laneway. The couple ended up selling the house a short time later, and the next purchaser (or rather her lawyer) was not prepared to accept the property with those minor defects.

The title insurance company helped to negotiate an acceptable abatement of the purchase price, which was covered by the title insurance policy. The insurer also paid the extra legal fees incurred by the sellers in dealing with the purchaser's lawyer.

The Rubber Cheque

One of the things lawyers do in processing a closing is check on the status of the tax account for the property being purchased. They find out how much the property taxes are for the year, how much of that the seller has paid and then compare that to how much the seller should have paid based on the number of days out of the year that the seller has owned the house. If there is a difference (and there almost always is) one way or another, the sum is "adjusted" on the closing. In other words, if the taxes are $3,000 for the year and the sale is closing at the end of June, then the seller would owe $1,500 in taxes to the local municipality (half of the year's taxes). If they have paid $1,400, then on the closing the buyer would get a credit for $100 for the unpaid taxes since the buyer will have to pay whatever is owing to the municipality. Conversely, if the seller paid $1,600, then they would have overpaid by $100 — the buyer owes them that $100 — which is adjusted for on closing.

In a recent case, a seller owed the local municipality $2,600 for taxes up to the closing date of his sale. The deal involved a short two-week closing. The seller knew that the buyer's lawyer would check the status of the tax account, so shortly after the deal was signed, he went to the City Hall and paid the city $3,000 by cheque. The city clerk accepted the check and entered the payment into the computer system. The next day, the lawyer acting for the buyer checked the status of the city taxes. On receipt of that request, the city clerk went to the same system and up came the $400 overpayment. The clerk reported this to the lawyer, who then, on closing, adjusted by having his client pay the seller back for the $400 overpayment. The problem occurred when the cheque given to the city by the seller bounced. The city clerk, upon realizing that the cheque was not valid, went back to the system and re-entered the credit — removing the payment and showing the original $2,600 owing. Did they bother telling the buyer's lawyer about this when they first found out? Of course not! It's City Hall: one hand does not necessarily know what the other is doing. In the end, the innocent buyer received a letter from the city several weeks after closing asking for the $2,600. The city can do this because a debt for taxes runs with the land; in other words, the municipality is entitled to look to whoever owns the property for satisfaction of the debt.

The buyer received the letter and immediately called his lawyer to complain. The lawyer instantly figured out what had happened. In the absence of a title insurance policy, the innocent buyer would have to chase down the seller and sue for the money back. In this case, fortunately for the buyer, there was title insurance in place. One of the items of coverage included with a title policy is coverage for errors in municipal records. In this case, the record given the lawyer for the buyer to the effect that there was a $400 overpayment was not correct. The coverage was in place and the title company paid the municipality immediately (within a day or two). The title company then has the right to pursue its remedies against the bad guy, the seller who wrote the bad cheque. The deductible on the claim? Nothing — there isn't any deductible on title insurance claims.

Hidden Renovations

A couple bought a single-family house. One of the features they liked was the fact that the house had a recently completed small addition. Their lawyer knew this and did all the right searches, including a check to see if the seller obtained a permit for the addition. The response from the local municipality was that a permit had been issued, all the necessary inspections had been done, and the file was closed. The deal then closed uneventfully.

Somehow, something about the way the addition was built bothered the new owners and after a while they called the municipal building inspector to come by and check it. The inspector dropped a bombshell on them when he told them that the previous owners had done considerable extra work that was outside the scope of the building permit. The permit was for the construction of a small crawlspace; the previous owners had constructed a full basement and concealed that work from the building inspector. To make matters worse, the work that was done was structurally unsound and the inspector issued a work order that required immediate attention. The structure was in danger of imminent collapse, and the family was told to take their valuables out of the room that was above the basement addition.

Fortunately for the family, their purchase was title insured. The policy had coverage for having to remove or remedy a part of the structure because that part was built without obtaining a building permit from the proper government office or agency. The cost to make the structure sound was over $25,000!

They'll Even Buy the House If They Have To

One item of coverage relates to marketability of a property that has been title insured. A good example of this happened recently when a house that was title insured went up for sale. The new buyers, after signing the agreement of purchase and sale but before closing, raised concerns about two portions of the seller's land that had encroachments of pavement onto it. In other words, there were two spots where the neighbour's concrete pavement actually sat over onto the seller's property. The new buyers wanted the encroachment removed and were concerned that the neighbour might have acquired some rights to the property being purchased through something known as possessory title. That is a form of title that one acquires through possession, not a title deed. The bottom line was that this was a big headache for the new buyers who, because of the problem, ultimately refused to close the deal. The seller put forward a claim to the title insurer, who responded by buying the house! The insurer paid the seller what the proceeds would have been, after the mortgage, and assumed the mortgage and took title themselves. The insurer then remarketed the property and was able to sell it.

Near Condo Disaster

A single mother bought an inexpensive condominium, and her lawyer proceeded to close the deal. One of the searches lawyers do when acting for condominium buyers is a search of the status of the condominium corporation's finances. If the finances are weak, and there is not enough money set aside to pay for major repairs, the condo corporation can charge the cost of repairs back to the unit owners. When buying a condominium, you really want to know whether that is likely to happen. In Ontario, lawyers get a certificate called a status certificate (formerly known as estoppel) that depicts the condo corporation's finances and, very importantly, advises whether any special assessments are planned to pay for major repairs.

In this particular case, the condo corporation issued an estoppel certificate, but neglected to mention a special assessment. In fact, the estoppel they issued was clear — no arrears or special assessments were planned — and 10 days later, they issued the charge for what in the end came to $20,000! That sum was very large in relation to the value of the unit. The buyer could, in theory, have sued the condominium management corporation for misrepresentation, but that would have involved lawyers and she simply could not afford justice, Canadian style. Fortunately for her, her lawyer title insured her deal and recognized that the policy provided coverage for errors in the estoppel certificate. The claim was made and paid. Her cost for the disaster? Nothing — there is no deductible for this type of claim.

Absent Permits

Many people assume that just because renovations have been done to a house, the proper permits were obtained and everything is in good working order. Some people believe, falsely, that if the work is obviously new, then a home inspection is not necessary. In a recent claim, homebuyers noticed some obvious problems with the wood stove, plumbing system, and furnace after moving into their new house. It turned out that the previous owner had not bothered to obtain proper permits for the work done. Because of that, no inspection ever took place to ensure that the work complied with applicable building codes. When the inspection was done, it became apparent that, in fact, the work did not comply with the building code. Coverage was available to the new owners because the work had been done without permits. The policy covered the cost of obtaining the necessary permits and the cost of making the work comply with the local building code.

Do You Feel Lucky?

All the above stories have one thing in common: innocent homebuyers who, through no fault of their own, were exposed to significant financial loss. Where title insurance was used, financial disaster was averted. The bottom line is that a title insured closing offers more protection than one that relies merely on the lawyer's opinion on title. Many seasoned real estate lawyers know that and insist on placing the coverage as part of the way they do business because they want what is truly best for their clients.

I was watching an old Clint Eastwood movie the other day. In one famous scene, he asks the bad guy, "You have to ask yourself... do you feel lucky?" That is a very good question homebuyers who don't have their purchase title insured should ask themselves. Is this a chance you want to take?

With any financial decision, it is always prudent to do a cost benefit analysis. In other words, compare the cost of something against what the benefits are likely to be. When it comes to the issue of title insurance, the simple truth is that no matter how you slice it, there is no compelling reason not to obtain it. In many parts of the country, just having your lawyer use it as part of the process will result in it being either cost neutral or result in a cost savings. If you avoid the whole survey issue, again a cost savings will likely result. Even where the money saved through the avoidance of unnecessary searches or the survey does not match the cost of the policy, the value in terms of peace of mind in not having to worry about something as serious as fraud is priceless. Nobody wants to have to live through a several-year lawsuit defending what for most people is their most valuable asset — that is, unless they feel lucky and want to take that chance.

Things To Keep in Mind

Bad things can and do happen all the time that threaten your investment, but you can get yourself some protection in the form of mortgage life, fire, and title insurance.

- If you have children or other dependents who would suffer financially should you die, then you are well advised to have some form of life insurance.

- You can purchase mortgage life insurance directly from your lender or buy life insurance from a private insurance company; mortgage life insurance from a lender is generally cheaper but has some restrictions as to how the money is paid out that you may not like.

- Life insurance from an insurance company basically comes in two forms: term or permanent.

- Term life insurance is insurance for a specified period of time; when the term expires, it is up to you to renew, and once you reach 65 to 70 years old, you cannot buy term insurance.

- Within term insurance, there are two basic types of policies — level term (in which the premium you pay and the benefit on death are fixed for the duration of the term) and decreasing or declining term (in which the benefit declines at a fixed rate over the term).

- Permanent insurance is more complex than term insurance and has a savings element to it. It is more expensive, but the coverage is for life and has no limitation based on term.

- A permanent variable life insurance policy provides that a portion of what you pay as a premium goes into a cash value account, the money is then invested in different types of securities. You are allowed to borrow from the policy, but you are not able to withdraw money during your lifetime.

- A permanent universal life policy is made up of an insurance and a savings portion, and you can borrow against the value of the policy or withdraw money from it.

- Lenders insist that you have fire insurance to cover the property *from the day of closing*. It is up to you to arrange for the coverage and to have a binder letter provided to your lawyer so that he or she can prove coverage to the lender who will insist on that proof before advancing mortgage money.

- Title insurance is something everyone should obtain. Remember, it is only available through your lawyer. Many lawyers today refuse to conduct a closing without it because it offers you broader protection than the lawyer alone was able to offer in the past.

Common sense dictates that it is smart to protect your investment with appropriate insurance. If you have decided to be smart about the way you buy or sell, mortgage and invest, doesn't it pay to be smart about protection too?

7

Show Me
the Money!

*"Hell, there are no rules here — we're
trying to accomplish something."*

— THOMAS EDISON

Many people never seem to be all that certain as to what to do with their money. Years ago, I simply kept what money I had in GICs and rolled them over every year or so when they came due. The money grew but at a steady, slow rate. Then everyone told me that I should have a financial adviser. So, I got hold of one through my bank and listened to his complex plan. (I should have asked for a good adviser.) He seemed to know what he was talking about, however, so I gave him all my money and the money I was saving for my kids. In about five months he invested things in such a way that 25% of the value of my portfolio was lost. I was quite upset. Suddenly my boring GICs didn't look so bad after all. Maybe they did not keep pace with inflation, but at least they grew. I then hired another adviser and transferred all the money to his firm. The new guy's performance was also disappointing. Nothing has gone up dramatically, much of it has dropped in value (can you spell NORTEL?), and the only bright side is that when I do the opposite of what he says, I seem to do well. Maybe I just don't have the right adviser or maybe I don't have the stomach for all that volatility.

Just about everyone I know who invests in the stock market has told me at one point or another that they wish they had just broken even on their investments. If that's the case, why bother to start?

What has served me well, and been the saving grace in all this, are the houses that we have bought, lived in, and sold over the years. Generally, we have bought older homes in desirable neighbourhoods, renovated them, lived in them for a while, and sold them. That very simple, almost unconscious strategy has created the cornerstone of my retirement fund. Nothing fancy in that strategy.

Once you buy a house, what is the best way to manage your money? Should you focus on paying off the mortgage? Should you carry the mortgage and use any surplus funds for investments in the stock market or to make RRSP contributions? Should you try to hold your mortgage in your RRSP? Gurus abound — who to listen to?

I'm not an economist. I do not have an accounting or financial planning background, and I don't sell mutual funds. But I do understand the basics.

I understand that it's reasonable to look back over the last 20 or 30 years and see what has happened to house values and compare that to how the stock market has performed. I understand that many investment strategies sound great, but require investment discipline that no one I know possesses. I understand that most people who buy houses and have mortgages pay the mortgage each month, as a forced savings plan, and as they do that, the debt gets smaller and their equity in the house grows. I understand that some economic theories are so qualified (on the one hand blah blah blah, and on the other hand yada yada yada) that it's difficult to draw any conclusions from them. I understand that numbers on a piece of paper provide some comfort, but not as much as a warm fireplace and a nice home.

This chapter examines these issues, reviews some "expert" advice, and outlines some interesting facts and viewpoints to consider as part of your overall investment strategy. Your house can be your largest financial asset. How you manage your money while owning that house is therefore of the utmost importance. One way to avoid devastating money-management errors is to have all the facts and views, enabling your decision to be informed.

How To Be House Rich

You've bought a house (hopefully following the advice in this book) and are now faced with the important question: How do you manage your money so as to maximize chances of growth? Should you pay down the mortgage, or invest the surplus in an RRSP or other forms of investments?

There is a simple way to determine this, according to Dr. Moshe Milevsky, Ph.D. (Finance Professor, The Schulich School of Business at York University and Executive Director, The Individual Finance and Insurance Decisions Centre). If you have an outstanding mortgage, and extra room in your RRSP, then you should compare the interest rate on your mortgage to what you expect to earn on the investments in your RRSP. As Milevsky puts it, "The higher expectation wins." For example, if you are paying a 7% interest on your mortgage, but you believe you can earn more than 7% in your RRSP, then go ahead and invest in the RRSP Mutual Fund or RRSP GIC. If, on the other hand, you are doubtful you can earn the 7% within the RRSP, then go ahead and pay down your mortgage. In other words, since both interest paid on mortgages and interest paid to borrow money for an RRSP are not tax-deductible, the decision comes down to rates of return, and nothing else.

That certainly makes sense and is a good starting point to consider. I asked other financial experts for their advice. The responses I received essentially fell into two categories: (1) paying down the mortgage quickly and (2) carrying the mortgage and diversifying.

Paying Down the Mortgage Quickly

People who follow this path often remember the dark days of super-high interest rates of the late '80s. Many lost their homes when the rates rose on their debt so much that they could not afford their mortgage any longer. People who remember that may see value in lowering their debt as quickly as possible as a hedge against something like that happening again. But other people see it as a simple strategy.

According to John Kelly, Director for Century 21, Financial Services Canada, "investment into your mortgage is a great way to be mortgage free earlier and save thousands of dollars in interest." He suggests looking at your overall debt load and working at paying it down in order of highest interest: the first line of attack should be against all higher interest debt such as credit cards and personal loans, and the second line of attack should be accelerated payment of the mortgage as a high-return, risk-free investment.

Keep in mind that mortgage interest on your primary residence (as well as credit cards) is paid with after-tax dollars. Income tax is first deducted from your gross employment earnings, and then mortgage interest payments are paid out of your remaining after-tax income. Since we are talking about after-tax earnings, investing in your mortgage can result in substantial savings and excellent returns on investment.

Just like Dr. Milevsky, Kelly feels that it makes financial sense to pay down your mortgage over investing in competing alternatives such as stocks, bonds, or term deposits, if the rate of return you get from these alternatives is lower than the rate of return received from investing in your mortgage. There is no sense in earning 5% from a GIC if you have to pay 7% interest on your mortgage: your net shortfall is 2%. The wiser investment would be to invest the GIC amount into your mortgage, saving 7% and avoiding the 2% shortfall. He suggests comparing the before- and after-tax rates; however, watch what you are comparing. If you compare the interest savings resulting from mortgage pre-payment (essentially your rate of return) with the returns promised from investment in a speculative stock, you are not comparing apples with apples. The return rate from paying down your mortgage is certain, while the return on stock investments is not.

Rick Lunny, Senior Vice President Real Estate Secured Lending, TD Canada Trust, adds, "If you're weighing the pros of paying down your mortgage vs. investing elsewhere, remember that the compound nature of interest works both ways. Just as a small nest egg can grow to a substantial sum over the years, so too can you save thousands by making early or extra mortgage payments. In other words, you are wise to pay down your mortgage as quickly as possible. You can reduce your after-tax interest costs by almost $50,000 by paying down your $100,000, 7% per annum mortgage over 15 years instead of the usual 25 years. Even if, like most of us, you are stretched to the max when you first purchase your home, as little as an extra $1,000 a year in principal payment will see your mortgage paid off in 19 years compared to 25 years and save about $30,000 in borrowing costs."

It's easy to see the effect the pre-payment you feel you can afford will have on the amortization period and overall interest costs of your mortgage. All you have to do is check one of the online calculators, such as **www.cimbl.ca.**, plug in the numbers, and view the results.

Lunny encourages consumers to build a savings nest egg for unforeseen expenses and suggests that saving with mutual funds can be a good way to diversify your investments. He points out that homeowners can even re-borrow against their home at preferential interest rates in the future for investment purposes, on which interest will then be tax deductible for qualified investments.

Lastly, Lunny feels that "investing your hard-earned dollars is more complicated than mortgage payment amortization schedules or investment return comparisons. It should be a personal decision based on your stage in life, economic circumstances and established values."

Carrying the Mortgage and Diversifying

Many experts seem to agree with the old saying about there being value in diversity. They feel that homeowners are well-advised to carry their mortgage and invest in RRSPs in order to diversify. There is value in not having all of your eggs in one basket; a proper investment portfolio should have a home as well as mutual funds in it.

Peter Norman, Vice-President at Clayton Research (a firm of urban and real estate economists), thinks that paying off your mortgage slowly may actually make you wealthier than paying it off quickly. According to Mr. Norman, "Mortgage rates are generally lower than returns generated from investing." As mentioned earlier, many families lost their homes in the late '80s because they could not afford to make the high interest rate payments. This fear inspires many to put their extra money into paying down their mortgages, and, according to Norman, "for high-ratio mortgage holders, this strategy may be prudent." However, many mortgage holders are not high ratio, and for them, "the risks of a spike in interest rates are remote, and current interest rates, which are in the 6 to 8% range, are presently well below potential returns generated by financial markets."

A determination of a trend necessarily involves looking over the long term. The fact is that in the 10 years leading up to 2000, the average return on the TSE 300 index was 10% per year. This compares to an average mortgage cost of 7.2% per year over the same time period. Because of this, according to Norman, "while there is certainly short-term variability, investors with their eye on long-term results should generally take any extra cash on hand to their investor, rather than their mortgage holder."

Most Canadians do not invest the maximum into their RRSPs. Because of this, Norman feels that there are tax advantages to investing rather than paying off the mortgage. For example, "only 55% of Canadian households invest into their RRSPs and most of those do a rather weak job of it: half of households who do have RRSPs have less than $20,000 invested. RRSP investments are tax deductible, whereas there is no direct tax advantage to paying down a mortgage. To a person in Ontario in the middle tax bracket, this means an implied 35% bonus on his or her investments. Taking the TSE index as an example of one possible RRSP investment, that 10% annual return becomes 13.5%. Even a 5-year GIC, which had an average annual return of 5.9% over the past 10 years, gets a boost up to 7.9% if it is in an RRSP. The essentially risk-free 5-year GIC, invested within an RRSP, pays out more in interest than the family would incur through their mortgage."

Peter Vukanovich, CA, President of GE Capital Mortgage Insurance Canada, agrees that "paying off a mortgage is a form of forced savings. People will have a monthly shelter cost but if they purchase a home using a mortgage instead of renting, once the mortgage is paid off they have a valuable asset. Hence a portion of the mortgage payment that they make each month is a form of savings."

Having said that, Vukanovich points out that diversity in the balance of investments one has is very wise since, "no one has the absolute ability to accurately predict the future and how unforeseen occurrences might affect an investment." Those words ring true. Moreover, "every investor is different and they must determine the right mix of risk and reward as well as the right balance of real estate, stocks, bonds, securities, and funds. However, there is one thing for certain: when that mix is developed with a 20-plus year time frame, almost all investors can build wealth."

David Karas (CFP, RFP, RFC), is a leading financial planning expert, author, columnist, and broadcaster. He feels that," in the simplest terms, residential real estate is shelter. What makes it an investment is inflation. Without inflation, all homes would be worth the purchase price less depreciation, somewhat similar to a used car." That's an interesting way of looking at things. Karas feels that "the biggest mistake you can make with real estate is owning only real estate. The second biggest mistake is not owning real estate."

According to Karas, owning real estate as part of your investment portfolio is essential for three reasons:

1. It acts as a forced savings plan, in that each month that you make the mortgage payment, you increase your net worth.

2. If you don't own, then you are renting, and if you are renting, then you are paying off someone else's mortgage.

3. Inflation will lower the cost of the purchase you made 10 to 25 years ago.

As Karas says, "remember that the house you buy actually does not increase in value; instead, the money you purchase it with depreciates in purchasing power. In simplest terms, real estate ownership offsets the ravages of inflation."

Karas also points out that there are three fundamental rules of real estate. The first rule is that you should buy real estate and pay off the mortgage in a reasonable time, preferring 15-year amortizations over 25.

The second rule is to never leave your money in the house. Karas advises, "always take the equity back out of the house and reinvest it back into an investment where its growth will outperform the potential growth of the home. A good investment is a diversified portfolio of equity mutual funds. This alternative investment can outperform the rate of appreciation of real estate (usually the inflation rate) because you will be investing in businesses that actually do something other than provide shelter."

The third rule is that you should always convert non-deductible debts (such as a mortgage) to a deductible debt (such as an investment loan). By doing this you will have the government paying up to half the loan cost for you (the loan amount times your marginal tax rate times the loan interest cost). You can do this by mortgaging the equity in your home to provide qualified investment funds. Karas neatly explains this point with the following example.

John (age 45 and in the 47.9% Ontario income tax bracket) bought a house 10 years ago for $225,000. The house appreciated at slightly less than the rate of inflation; namely, only 2.5%, so now it is worth $288,019.

He bought the house with a little more than 30% down at that time and took out a mortgage loan of $150,000 at a loan rate of 7%, calculated semi-annually, to complete the purchase. His mortgage was set up on a 15-year amortization basis, so he has maintained an accelerated schedule of principal pay down over the last 10 years. Today he owes $67,828 on the mortgage.

As part of his recommendations, John's financial planner suggested that John take a $100,000 line of credit on the home and invest it in 10 high-quality mutual funds. The interest rate on the line of credit is 7.5% and the repayment terms require that interest only be paid monthly.

Here's what happens. The interest on the debt is tax deductible. Instead of paying $625.00 per month, his actual after-tax interest cost is $325.63. The government pays the balance of the interest cost ($299.37 per month). If John wants, he can get his tax refund monthly as opposed to waiting until the end of the year for his refund.

He has two options. If he can service the payments for the loan out of pocket, by the time he is 65 he will have $366,096 at an 8% investment return following repayment of the $100,000 loan principal. At 12% he would have $864,629.

If he wants to employ a systematic withdrawal plan (SWP), he can have the investment make its own interest payments by selling a portion of the investment each month to pay the line of credit. If he does this he will have $179,620 at 8% or $565,096 at 12% following repayment of the loan principal. Obviously this strategy results in less growth because John sells part of the investment each month to service the interest costs. The advantage of this strategy is that his day-to-day cash flow is not touched.

What would happen if John did nothing? If his house continued to grow at the 2.5% rate, its value would be $471,952 when John reaches 65 years of age. If he uses the line of credit and pays it himself, he would have $366,096 at 8% or $864,629 at 12%, plus he still has the house. This is a net worth improvement of between 177% and 283%.

If he employed a systematic investment plan and invested $325.63 per month (the amount he would otherwise be paying in interest on the loan) from age 45 to age 65, he would have $185,283 at 8% and $296,718 at 12%. At the higher rate of return, John would be significantly better off had he borrowed $100,000 to invest and let the investment make the loan interest payments. He would have $565,096 at 12% rate of return rather than $296,718, an improvement of 190%.

The numbers speak for themselves; Karas makes a compelling argument.

By way of summary, Karas adds, "You should buy a home. Live in it and enjoy it. Take your money out of it and buy other investments. Then buy RRSPs with the investment money you have earned from the money you borrowed from the home. You need to own a home."

Things To Keep in Mind

If I gave you my eyeglasses and said, "here, put them on, they will make you see better," you might wonder what I am talking about. Just because the glasses work for me does not mean that they will work for you. Everyone is a bit different. At the same time, we know that if you want to see better, then getting some kind of glasses is a good idea.

I think investment advice is a bit like that too. Everyone has needs that make him or her unique. There is no disputing that. Investment advice that works for me will not necessarily work for you. So you need to consider your own particular situation to assess the following.

- There are two basic routes to take for managing your money while owning a house: (1) paying down the mortgage quickly or (2) carrying the mortgage and diversifying (or a bit of both).

- Compare the interest rate on your mortgage to what you expect to earn on the investments in your RRSP to decide on which route to take.

- In order to pay down your mortgage quickly, look at your overall debt load and work at paying it down in order of highest interest: (1) credit cards and personal loans and (2) accelerated payment of your mortgage.

- Mortgage pre-payment has a remarkable effect on your overall interest payments. And savings in a mutual fund make an ideal savings nest egg to protect against unforeseen events.

- High-ratio borrowers should consider paying down their mortgage as a hedge against the effect of future interest rate increases. But homeowners who pay their mortgage off slowly and invest may actually end up wealthier than those who pay it off quickly. This is especially true for those who take advantage of available tax-reduction strategies, such as investing into an RRSP.

- Paying a mortgage is really a form of forced savings yet having diversity in your investments is very wise since, over time, all investments create wealth.

- Inflation makes a house an investment and owning real estate is an essential part of an investment portfolio. A three-pronged strategy includes buying real estate and paying off the mortgage in a reasonable time (15 years vs. 25); taking the equity back out of the house and reinvesting it into an investment where the growth will outperform that of the house; and converting non-deductible debts (e.g., mortgages) to deductible debts (e.g., investment loans).

Having come to this point in the book (unless you peeked at the end first), you should have gleaned essential information on all aspects of buying, owning, and selling a home. Armed with that information and insight, you are well-equipped to tackle the world of real estate. You can recognize some of the tricks of the trade of realtors and others whose paths may cross yours. In forming decisions on investments and the future financial well-being of you and your family, you know more of what to watch out for. It is my sincere hope that you profit from the knowledge you have gained from reading this book. Everyone has to live somewhere. And of all the risks in life, buying a home is one of the most sensible things to do. If done right, home ownership can be one of the most rewarding, too.

Appendix 1: Useful Web Sites

Banks

- **www.bmo.com** (Bank of Montreal)
- **www.scotiabank.ca** (Bank of Nova Scotia)
- **www.cibc.com** (Canadian Imperial Bank of Commerce)
- **www.nbc.ca** (National Bank of Canada)
- **www.royalbank.com** (Royal Bank of Canada)
- **www.tdbank.ca** (Toronto Dominion Canada Trust)
- **www.hsbc.ca** (HSBC)
- **www.citizens.com** (Citizens Bank of Canada)
- **www.laurentianbank.com** (Laurentian Bank of Canada)
- **www.manulife.com** (Manulife Bank of Canada)
- **www.ingdirect.ca** (ING Bank of Canada)
- **www.ethniki.gr** (National Bank of Greece)
- **www.bcibank.com** (Banca Commerciale Italiana of Canada)

Mortgage Brokers

- **www.cimbl.ca** (Canadian Institute of Mortgage Brokers and Lenders)
- **www.mortgageintelligence.ca** (Mortgage Intelligence)
- **www.mortgagecentre.com** (The Mortgage Centre)
- **www.multi-prets.com** or **www.tmacc.com** (Mortgage Alliance Canada)
- **www.hlcmortgages.com** (Home Loans Canada)

Realtors

- **www.remax.ca** (Re/Max)
- **www.royallepage.ca** (Royal Lepage)
- **www.coldwellbanker.ca** (Coldwell Banker)
- **www.century21.ca** (Century 21)
- **www.realtyworld.ca** (Realty World)

- www.prudential.com (Prudential)
- www.homelife.com (HomeLife Realty)
- www.bhg-real-estate.ca (Better Homes and Gardens)
- www.sutton.com (Sutton Group Realty)
- www.realtyexecutives.com (Realty Executives Canada)
- www.exitrealty.com (Exit Realty)

Title Insurers

- www.firstcanadiantitle.com (First Canadian Title)
- www.stewart.ca (Stewart Title Guaranty Co.)
- www.ctic.ca (Chicago Title, with links to Title Plus www.titleplus.ca)

Default Insurers (National Housing Act Insurers)

- www.gemortgage.ca (GE Capital)
- www.cmhc-schl.gc.ca (CMHC)

Miscellaneous Information Sites

- www.kormanturk.com (legal info.)
- www.homestore.ca (listings and great information)
- www.quicken.ca (great information)
- www.etrade.ca (great information)
- www.orea.com (Ontario Real Estate Association)
- www.crea.ca (Canadian Real Estate Association)
- www.mls.ca (Multiple Listing Service)
- www.nahb.com (U.S. site –National Association of Home Builders)
- www.newhomes.org (Greater Toronto Home Builders' Association)
- www.chba.ca (Canadian Home Builders' Association)
- www.ccra-adrc.gc.ca (Canada Customs and Revenue Agency, with details on government programs, specifically, www.ccra-adrc.gc.ca/menu/EmenuGOC.html [RRSP Plan])
- www.cahi.ca (Canadian Association of Home Inspectors — with links to provincial Associations)
- www.ashi.com (American Society of Home Inspectors)
- www.filogix.com (Filogix)

Appendix 2: Real Estate Associations and Boards

This section is reproduced through the kind courtesy of the Canadian Real Estate Association, **www.mls.ca/crea**

About CREA
Boards/Associations

The Canadian Real Estate Association
344 Slater Street, Suite 1600
Ottawa, ON K1R 7Y3
Tel.: (613) 237-7111, Fax: (613) 234-2567
Email: **info@crea.ca**

Alberta

The Alberta Real Estate Association
Suite 310, 2424-4th Street S.W.
Calgary, AB T2S 2T4
Tel.: (403) 228-6845, or 1-800-661-0231,
Fax: (403) 228-4360
www.abrea.ab.ca

Brooks Real Estate Board Co-
Operative Ltd.
Box 997
Brooks, AB T1R 1B8
Tel.: (403) 362-7000, Fax: (403) 362-2632

Calgary Real Estate Board
Co-Operative Ltd.
805 5th Avenue S.W.
Calgary, AB T2P 0N6
Tel.: (403) 263-0530, Fax: (403) 781-1307
Email: **inquiry@creb.com**
www.creb.com

Edmonton Real Estate Board Co-Operative
Listing Bureau
14220 112th Avenue, PO Box 25000
Edmonton, AB T5J 2R4
Tel.: (403) 451-6666, Fax: (403) 452-1135
Email: **mls@ereb.ab.ca**
www.mls.ca/board/edmonton

The Fort McMurray Real Estate Board
Co-Operative Listing Bureau
200 9908 Franklin Avenue
Fort McMurray, AB T9H 2K5
Tel.: (403) 791-1124, Fax: (403) 743-4724
www.cres.universal.ca/rnet/
cgi-bin/reb/gunREB/index.html

Grande Prairie Real Estate Board
10106 - 102nd Street
Grande Prairie, AB T8V 2V7
Tel.: (780) 532-4508, Fax: (780) 539-3515
Email: **gpmls@telusplanet.net**
www.gpmls.com

Lethbridge Real Estate Board Co-
Operative Ltd.
522 6th Street S.
Lethbridge, AB T1J 2E2
Tel.: (403) 328-8838, Fax: (403) 328-8906
Email: **lreb@telusplanet.net**
ww.mls.ca/boards/lethbridge

Lloydminster Real Estate Board
Association
203-5009 48th Street
Lloydminster, AB, T9V 0H9
Tel.: (780) 875-6939, Fax: (780) 875-5560

Medicine Hat Real Estate Board
Co-Operative Ltd.
403 4th Street S.E.
Medicine Hat, AB T1A 0K5
Tel.: (403) 526-2879, Fax: (403) 526-0307
Email: **mhreb@telusplanet.net**
www.mls.ca/boards/medicinehat

Northeastern Alberta Real Estate Board
Co-operative Ltd.
PO Box 1678, Lake Centre Plaza
Cold Lake, AB T9M 1P4
Tel.: (780) 594-5958, Fax: (780) 594-3181
Email: **neareb@jetnet.ab.ca**
www.celebrity.ca/rnet/
cgi-bin/reb/ab/northeastREB/
index.html?prob=ab

Red Deer and District Real Estate Board
Co-operative Ltd.
4922-45 Street
Red Deer, AB T4N 1K6
Tel.: (403) 343-0881, Fax: (403) 347-9080
Email: **rdreb@agt.net**
www.rdreb.ab.ca

West Central Alberta Real Estate Board
Foothills Bldg., 162 Athabasca Street
Hinton, AB T7V 2A4
Tel.: (403) 865-7511, Fax: (403) 865-7517

British Columbia

British Columbia Real Estate Association
309 - 1155 West Pender Street
Vancouver, BC V6E 2P4
Tel.: (604) 683-7702, Fax: (604) 683-8601
Email: **bcrea@helix.net**
www.bcrea.bc.ca

B.C. Northern Real Estate Board
2609 Queensway
Prince George, BC V2L 1N3
Tel.: (250) 563-1236, Fax: (250) 563-3637
Email: **carea@cariboo-rea.ba.ca**
www.mls.ca/boards/cariboo

Chilliwack & District Real Estate Board
Suite 201 - 9319 Nowell Street, Box 339
Chilliwack, BC V2P 6J4
Tel.: (604) 792-0912, Fax: (604) 792-6795
Email: **cadreb@uniserve.com**
www.mls.ca/boards/chilliwack

Fraser Valley Real Estate Board
15463 104th Avenue
Surrey, BC V3R 1N9
Tel.: (604) 930-7600, Fax: (604) 930-7625
Email: **mls@fvreb.bc.ca**
www.fvreb.bc.ca

Kamloops & District Real Estate
Association
101 - 418 St. Paul Street
Kamloops, BC V2C 2J6
Tel.: (250) 372-9411, Fax: (250) 828-1986
Email: **mail@ocis.net**
www.mls.ca/board/kamloops

Kootenay Real Estate Board
208 - 402 Baker Street, Box 590
Nelson, BC V1L 4H8
Tel.: (250) 352-5477, Fax: (250) 352-7184
Email: **kreb@netidea.com**

Northern Lights Real Estate Board
1101 103 Avenue
Dawson Creek, BC V1G 2G8
Tel.: (250) 782-2412, Fax: (250) 782-8574

Okanagan-Mainline Real Estate Board
1889 Spall Road
Kelowna, BC V1Y 4R2
Tel.: (250) 860-6292, Fax: (250) 860-7704
Email: **admin@omreb.com**
www.mls.ca/boards/okanaganmain

Powell River Sunshine Coast Real
Estate Board
4680 Willingdon Avenue
Powell River, BC V8A 2N4
Tel.: (604) 485-6944, Fax: (604) 485-6974

Real Estate Board of Greater Vancouver
2433 Spruce Street
Vancouver, BC V6H 4C8
Tel.: (604) 730-3000, Fax: (604) 730-3103
www.realtylink.org

South Okanagan Real Estate Board
Suite 3 - 212 Main Street
Penticton, BC V2A 5B2
Tel.: (250) 492-0626, Fax: (250) 493-0832
Email: **soreb@vip.net**
www.mls.ca/boards/southokanagan

Vancouver Island Real Estate Board
6374 Metral Drive, Box 719
Nanaimo, BC V9R 5M2
Tel.: (250) 390-4212, Fax: (250) 390-5014
Email: **vireb@vireb.com**
www.mls.ca/boards/vireb

Victoria Real Estate Board
3035 Nanaimo Street
Victoria, BC V8T 4W2
Tel.: (250) 385-7766, Fax: (250) 385-8773
Email: **vreb@vreb.org**
www.vreb.org

Manitoba

The Manitoba Real Estate Association
2nd Floor-1240 Portage Avenue
Winnipeg, MB R3G 0T6
Tel.: (204) 772-0405, Fax: (204) 775-3781
www.realestatemanitoba.com

Brandon Real Estate Board Inc.
907 Princess Avenue
Brandon, MB R7A 6E3
Tel.: (204) 727-4672, Fax: (204) 727-8331
www.breb.mb.ca

The Portage La Prairie Real Estate Board
112 Saskatchewan Avenue East
La Prairie, MB R1N 0L1
Tel.: (204) 857-4111, Fax: (204) 857-7207

The Winnipeg Real Estate Board
1240 Portage Avenue
Winnipeg, MB R3G 0T6
Tel.: (204) 786-8854, Fax: (204) 783-9447
Email: **mls@wreb.mb.ca**
www.wreb.mb.ca

Thompson Real Estate Board Inc.
c/o G.J. Sherry & Association (1987)Ltd.
25 Selkirk Avenue
Thompson, MB R8N 0M5
Tel.: (204) 677-4538, Fax: (204) 677-4530

New Brunswick

The New Brunswick Real Estate
Association
358 King Street, Suite 301
Fredericton, NB E3B 1E3
Tel.: (506) 459-8055, Fax: (506) 459-8057
Email: **nbrea@nbnet.nb.ca**

Saint John Real Estate Board Inc.
120 - 600 Main Street
Building "C," Hilyard Place
Saint John, NB E2K 1J5
Tel.: (506) 634-8772, Fax: (506) 634-8775
Email: **sjreb@nbnet.nb.ca**

The Greater Moncton Real Estate
Board Inc.
107 Cameron Street
Moncton, NB E1C 5Y7
Tel.: (506) 857-8200, Fax: (506) 857-1760
Email: **mls@nbnet.nb.ca**
www.mls.ca/boards/moncton

The Northern New Brunswick Real Estate
Board Inc.
PO Box 185, Suite 5, 360 Parkside Drive
Bathurst, NB E2A 3Z2
Tel.: (506) 548-3045, Fax: (506) 548-4002
Email: **nnbreb@nb.sympatico.ca**

The Real Estate Board of Fredericton
Area Inc.
544 Brunswick Street
Fredericton, NB E3B 1Y5
Tel.: (506) 458-8163, Fax: (506) 459-8922
Email: **freb01@nb.sympatico.ca**
www.brunnet.net/freb

Valley Real Estate Board Inc
56 Church Street
Edmunston, NB E3V 1J5
Tel.: (506) 735-5521, Fax: (506) 735-1852
www.valleyboard.com

Newfoundland

Newfoundland Real Estate Association
251 Empire Avenue
St. John's, NF A1C 3H9
Tel.: (709) 726-5110, Fax: (709) 726-4221

Central Newfoundland Real Estate Board
92 Elizabeth Drive, Suite 2
Gander, NF A1V 2W7
Tel.: (709) 256-7999, Fax: (709) 256-9221

Humber Valley Real Estate Board
PO Box 532
Corner Brook, NF A2H 6E6
Tel.: (709) 634-9400, Fax: (709) 643-3251

St. John's Real Estate Board
251 Empire Avenue, 2nd Floor
St. John's, NF A1C 3H9
Tel.: (709) 726-5110, Fax: (709) 726-4221
Email: **mls@thezone.net**

Nova Scotia

Nova Scotia Real Estate Association
7 Scarfe Court
Dartmouth, NS B3B 1W4
Tel.: (902) 468-2515, Fax: (902) 468-2533

Annapolis Valley Real Estate Board
PO Box 117, 2110 Highway 1
Auburn, NS B0P 1A0
Tel.: (902) 847-9336, Fax: (902) 847-9869
Email: **avreb@ns.sympatico.ca**

Association of the Northern Nova Scotia
Real Estate Board
25 Harmony Road
Truro, NS B2N 4X9
Tel.: (902) 893-3809, Fax: (902) 893-4533

Cape Breton Real Estate Board
15 Victoria Street
North Sydney, NS B2A 1G5
Tel.: (902) 794-1977, Fax: (902) 794-1977

Halifax-Dartmouth Real Estate Board
7 Scarfe Court
Dartmouth, NS B3B 1W4
Tel.: (902) 468-7681, Fax: (902) 468-7684
Email: **hdreb@istar.ca**
home.istar.ca/~hdreb

Highland Real Estate Board
PO Box 226
St. Peter's, NS B0E 3B0
Tel.: (902) 535-3228, Fax: (902) 535-2202

South Shore Real Estate Board
PO Box 81
Bridgewater, NS B4V 2W6
Tel.: (902) 543-7642, Fax: (902) 543-1290
Email: **ssreb@ns.sympatico.ca**

Yarmouth Real Estate Board
c/o Anchorage Better Homes & Gardens
12 Kirk Street
Yarmouth, NS B5A 1S7
Tel.: (902) 742-1060, Fax: (902) 742-0080

Northwest Territories

Yellowknife Real Estate Board
201 - 5204 50th Avenue
Yellowknife, NT X1A 1E2
Tel.: (867) 920-4624, Fax: (867) 873-6387
Email: **officecomp@ssimicro.com**

Ontario

Ontario Real Estate Association
99 Duncan Mill Road
Don Mills, ON M3B 1Z2
Tel.: (416) 445-9910, Fax: (416) 445-2644
Email: **info@orea.com**
www.orea.com

Bancroft District Real Estate Board
PO Box 1522, 141 Hastings Street North
(Upstairs)
Bancroft, ON K0L 1C0
Tel.: (613) 332-3842, Fax: (613) 332-3842
Email: **bdreb@mail.bancom.net**
www.bancroftrealestate.on.ca

Barrie and District Real Estate Board Inc.
85 Ellis Drive
Barrie, ON L4M 8Z3
Tel.: (705) 739-4650, Fax: (705) 721-9101
Email: **infr@Barrie-mls.on.ca**
www.barrie-mls.on.ca

Brantford Regional Real Estate Association
59 Roy Boulevard
Brantford, ON N3R 7K1
Tel.: (519) 753-0308, Fax: (519) 753-8638
Email: **brrea@worldchat.com**
www.mls.ca/boards/brantford

Chatham-Kent Real Estate Board
188 St. Clair Street, P.O. Box 384
Chatham, ON N7M 5K5
Tel.: (519) 352-4351, Fax: (519) 352-6938
Email: **ckreb@mnsi.net**
www.mls.ca/boards/chatham/home.htm

Cobourg-Port Hope District Real Estate
Board
Suite 23 - 1011 William Street, Victoria
Place
Cobourg, ON K9A 5J4
Tel.: (905) 372-8630, Fax: (905) 372-1443
Email: **cphreb@eagle.ca**
www.eagle.ca/realestate

Cornwall and District Real Estate Board
25 Cumberland Street
Cornwall, ON K6J 4G8
Tel.: (613) 932-6457, Fax: (613) 932-1687
www.mls.ca/boards/cornwall

Durham Region Real Estate Board
50 Richmond Street East, Unit 14
Oshawa, ON L1G 7C7
Tel.: (905) 723-8184, Fax: (905) 723-7531
Email: **drreb@durhamrealestate.org**

Georgian Triangle Real Estate Board
54 Third Street
Collingwood, ON L9Y 1K3
Tel.: (705) 445-7295, Fax: (705) 445-7253
Email: **realestate@georgian.net**
www.mls.ca/boards/georgiantriangle

Grey Bruce Real Estate Board
504-10th Street
Hanover, ON N4N 1R1
Tel.: (519) 364-3827 or 364-3864, Fax: (519)
364-6800
Email: **gbreb@sos.on.ca**
www.mls.ca/boards/greyb

Guelph and District Real Estate Board
400 Woolwich Street
Guelph, ON N1H 3X1
Tel.: (519) 824-7270, Fax: (519) 824-5510
Email: **gdreb@kw.igs.net**

Hamilton-Burlington and District Real
Estate Board
505 York Boulevard
Hamilton, ON L8R 3K4
Tel.: (905) 529-8101, Fax: (905) 529-4349
Email: **hbdreb@hbdreb.on.ca**
www.hbdreb.on.ca

Huron Real Estate Board
60 East Street
Goderich, ON N7A 1N3
Tel.: (519) 524-4191, Fax: (519) 524-5093
www.mls.ca/boards/huron

Kingston and Area Real Estate Association
720 Arlington Park Place
Kingston, ON K7M 8H9
Tel.: (613) 384-0880, Fax: (613) 384-0863
Email: **karea@king.igs.net**

Kitchener-Waterloo Real Estate Board Inc
540 Riverbend Drive
Kitchener, ON N2K 3S2
Tel.: (519) 576-1400, Fax: (519) 741-5364
Email: **kwreb@kwreb.on.ca**
www.mls.ca/boards/kwreb

Lindsay and District Real Estate Board
31 Kent Street East
Lindsay, ON K9V 2C3
Tel.: (705) 324-4515, Fax: (705) 324-3916
Email: **lindsayboard@sympatico.ca**

London and St. Thomas Real Estate Board
342 Commissioners Road West
London, ON N6J 1Y3
Tel.: (519) 641-1400, Fax: (519) 641-1419
Email: **lstreb@wwdc.com**
realtors.mls.ca/london

Midland-Penetang District Real Estate
Board
PO Box 805
Midland, ON L4R 4P4
Tel.: (705) 526-8706, Fax: (705) 526-0701
Email: **mpdreb@bconnex.net**

Mississauga Real Estate Board
3355 The Collegeway, Unit 29
Mississauga, ON L5L 5T3
Tel.: (905) 608-6732, Fax: (905) 608-0045
www.realestate.ca/toronto/home.htm

Muskoka Real Estate Board
18 Chaffey Street
Huntsville, ON P1H 1K7
Tel.: (705) 788-1504, Fax: (705) 788-2040
Email: **mreb@vianet.on.ca**

Niagara Falls – Fort Erie Real Estate
Association
PO Box 456, 4411 Portage Road
Niagara Falls, ON L2E 6V2
Tel.: (905) 356-7593, Fax: (905) 356-3044

North Bay Real Estate Board
926 Cassells Street
North Bay, ON P1B 4A8
Tel.: (705) 472-6812, Fax: (705) 472-0529
Email: **nbreb@onlink.net**

Orangeville and District Real Estate Board
228 Broadway Avenue
Orangeville, ON L9W 1K5
Tel.: (519) 941-4547, Fax: (519) 941-8482

Orillia and District Real Estate Board Inc.
100 Coldwater Street East, PO Box 551
Orillia, ON L3V 6K2
Tel.: (705) 325-9958, Fax: (705) 325-0605
Email: **oriloreb@bconnex.net**
www.mls.ca/boards/orillia

Owen Sound and District Real Estate
Board
653-2nd Avenue East
Owen Sound, ON N4K 2G7
Tel.: (519) 371-1922, Fax: (519) 376-8465
Email: **owensreb@log.on.ca**

Parry Sound Real Estate Board
33 James Street
Parry Sound, ON P2A 1T6
Tel.: (705) 746-4020, Fax: (705) 746-2955
Email: **psreb@vianet.on.ca**

Peterborough Real Estate Board Inc.
Box 1330, 273 Charlotte Street
Peterborough, ON K9J 7H5
Tel.: (705) 745-5724, Fax: (705) 745-9377
Email: **info@peterbororealestate.com**
www.mls.ca/boards/peterborough

Quinte and District Real Estate Board
General Delivery, PO Box 128
Cannifton, ON K0K 1K0
Tel.: (613) 969-7873, Fax: (613) 962-1851
Email: **quinte.mls@reach.net**
www.quinterealestate.on.ca

Real Estate Board of Cambridge Inc.
75 Ainslie Street North
Cambridge, ON N1R 3J7
Tel.: (519) 623-3660, Fax: (519) 623-8253
Email: **office@cambridge.realestate-
board.net**
www.mgl.ca/~rebcamb

Real Estate Board of Ottawa-Carleton
1826 Woodward Drive
Ottawa, ON K2C 0P7
Tel.: (613) 225-2240, Fax: (613) 225-6420
www.ottawarealestate.org

Renfrew County Real Estate Board
377 Isabella St.
Pembroke, ON K8A 5T4
Tel.: (613) 735-5840, Fax: (613) 735-0405
www.ottawarealestate.org

Rideau-St. Lawrence Real Estate Board
1275 Kensington Parkway, Unit 12
Brockville, ON K6V 6C3
Tel.: (613) 342-3103, Fax: (613) 342-1637
Email: **rideau@recorder.ca**

Sarnia-Lambton Real Estate Board
555 Exmouth Street
Sarnia, ON N7T 5P6
Tel.: (519) 336-6871, Fax: (519) 344-1928
Email: **slreb@ebtech.net**

Sault Ste. Marie Real Estate Board
498 Queen Street East, Suite 1
Sault Ste. Marie, ON P6A 1Z8
Tel.: (705) 949-4560, Fax: (705) 949-5935

Simcoe and District Real Estate Board
44 Young Street
Simcoe, ON N3Y 1Y5
Tel.: (519) 426-4454, Fax: (519) 426-9330
Email: **realsim@kwic.com**

St. Catharines District Real Estate Board
116 Niagara Street
St. Catharines, ON L2R 4L4
Tel.: (905) 684-9459, Fax: (905) 687-7010
Email: **scdreb@vaxxine.com**
www.mlsniagara.com

Sudbury Real Estate Board
190 Elm Street West
Sudbury, ON P3C 1V3
Tel.: (705) 673-3388, Fax: (705) 673-3197
Email: **sreb@vianet.on.ca**

The Brampton Real Estate Board
1625 Steeles Avenue East
Brampton, ON L6T 4T7
Tel.: (905) 791-9913, Fax: (905)791-9430
www.realestate.ca/toronto/home.htm

The Haliburton District Real Estate Board
Box 99
Haliburton, ON K0M 2S0
Tel.: (705) 457-9093, Fax: (705) 457-9094
Email: **hdreb@halhinet.com**

The Oakville Milton and District Real
Estate Board
125 Navy Street
Oakville, ON LJ6 2Z5
Tel.: (905) 844-6491, Fax: (905) 844-6699
Email: **hdreb@halhinet.com**
www.omdreb.on.ca

The Perth County Real Estate Board
91 Brunswick Street
Stratford, ON N5A 3L9
Tel.: (519) 271-6870, Fax: (519)271-3040
Email: **pcreb@quadro.net**
www.quadro.net/~perthreb

Thunder Bay Real Estate Board
1135 Barton Street
Thunder Bay, ON P7B 5N3
Tel.: (807) 623-8422, Fax: (807) 623-0375

Tillsonburg District Real Estate Board
Box 35, 1 Library Lane
Tillsonburg, ON N4G 4H3
Tel.: (519) 842-9361, Fax: (519) 688-6850
Email: **tburgreb@kwic.com**

Timmins Real Estate Board
7 Balsam Street South
Timmins, ON P4N 2C7
Tel.: (705) 268-5451, Fax: (705) 264-6420
Email: **treb@vianet.on.ca**

Toronto Real Estate Board
1400 Don Mills Road
Don Mills, ON M3B 3N1
Tel.: (416) 443-8100, Fax: (416) 443-0797
www.realestate.ca/toronto/home.htm

Welland District Real Estate Board
706 East Main Street
Welland, ON L3B 3Y4
Tel.: (905) 735-3624, Fax: (905) 735-8722
Email: **realwell@itcanada.com**
www.mls.ca/boards/welland/
home.htm

Windsor – Essex County Real Estate Board
3005 Marentette Avenue
Windsor, ON N8X 4G1
Tel.: (519) 966-6432, Fax: (519) 966-4469
Email: **info@WindsorRealEstate.com**
www.windsorrealestate.com

Woodstock-Ingersoll and District Real
Estate Board
65 Springbank, Unit 6
Woodstock, ON, N4S 8V8
Tel.: (519) 539-3616, Fax: (519) 539-1975
Email: **widreb@oxford.net**

York Region Real Estate Board
27 Main Street North
Newmarket, ON L3Y 3Z6
Tel.: (905) 895-7624, Fax: (905) 895-9216
Email: **mail@yrreb.com**
www.realestate.ca/toronto/home.htm

Prince Edward Island

Prince Edward Island Real Estate
Association
75 St. Peter's Road
Charlottetown, PE C1A 5N7
Tel.: (902) 368-8451, Fax: (902) 894-9487

Quebec

Fédération des Chambres Immobilières du
Québec
600 chemin du Golf
Ile-des-Soeurs, QC H3E 1A8
Tel.: (514) 762-0212, Fax: (514) 762-0365

Chambre immobilière de Québec
990 av Holland
Québec, QC G1S 3T1
Tel.: (418) 688-3362, Fax: (418) 688-3577
Email: **courrier@ciq.qc.ca**

Chambre immobilière de l'Abitibi-
Témiscamingue Inc.
80 Monseigneur Tessier est, Bureau 201
Rouyn-Noranda, QC J9X 3B9
Tel.: (819) 762-1777, Fax: (819) 762-4030
Email: **ciat@cablevision.qc.ca**
www.ciat.qc.ca

Chambre immobilière de l'Estrie Inc.
22 rue Robidoux
Sherbrooke, QC J1J 2W1
Tel.: (819) 566-7616, Fax: (819) 566-7688
Email: **cie@abacom.com**

Chambre immobilière de l'Outaouais Inc.
197 boul St-Josepsh
Hull, QC J8Y 3X2
Tel.: (819) 771-5221, Fax: (819) 771-8715
www.immeuble.outaouais.q

Chambre immobilière de la Haute Yamaska
Inc.
96, rue Principale, bureau 104
Granby, QC J2G 2T4
Tel.: (450) 378-6702, Fax: (450) 375-5268
Email: **cihy@sympatico.ca**

Chambre immobilière de la Mauricie Inc.
1640, 6e rue, Suite 102
Trois-Rivières, QC G8Y 5B8
Tel.: (819) 379-9081, Fax: (819) 379-9262
Email: **immo.mauricie@tr.cgocable.ca**

Chambre immobilière de Lanaudière Inc.
765, boul. Manseau
Joliette, QC J6E 2E8
Tel.: (450) 759-8511, Fax: (450) 759-6557
Email: **cil@citenet.net**

Chambre immobilière de St-Hyacinthe Inc.
CP 667
St-Hyacinthe, QC J2S 7P5
Tel.: (450) 799-2210, Fax: (450) 799-2211

Chambre immobilière des Laurentides
555 boul Ste-Adele, Bureau 204
Ste-Adele, QC J8B 1A7
Tel.: (450) 229-3511, Fax: (450) 229-3812
Email: **cil@cedep.net**
www.mls.ca/boards/laurentides

Chambre immobilière du Centre du
Québec Inc.
355 boul St-Joseph, Local 46
Drummondville, QC J2C 2B1
Tel.: (819) 477-1033, Fax: (819) 474-7913
Email: **chambre@cgocable.ca**

Chambre immobilière du Grand Montréal
600 ch du Golf
Ile-des-Soeurs, QC H3E 1A8
Tel.: (514) 762-2440, Fax: (514) 762-1490
Email: **cigm@cigm.qc.ca**
www.mls.ca/boards/montreal

Chambre immobilière du Saguenay-Lac-St-
Jean Inc.
2655 boul. du Royaume, Bureau 490
Jonquière, QC G7S 4S9
Tel.: (418) 548-8808, Fax: (418) 548-2588
Email:
chambre@immobiliersaguenay.com
www.immobiliersaguenay.com

Chambre immobilière Est du Québec Inc.
216 rue de la Cathedrale, Bureau 6
Rimouski, QC G5L 5J2
Tel.: (418) 723-5393, Fax: (418) 725-5393

Saskatchewan

The Saskatchewan Real Estate Association
231 Robin Crescent
Saskatoon, SK S7L 6M8
Tel.: (306) 373-3350, Fax: (306) 373-5377

Association of Battlefords Realtors
501-1101-101st St., PO Box 611
North Battleford, SK S9A 2Y7
Tel.: (306) 445-6300, Fax: (306) 445-9020

Association of Regina Realtors Inc.
1854 McIntyre Street
Regina, SK S4P 2P9
Tel.: (306) 791-2700, Fax: (306) 781-7940
Email: **rrea@cableregina.com**
www.reginarealtors.com

Estevan Real Estate Board
Box 445
Estevan, SK S4A 2A4
Tel.: (306) 634-7885, Fax: (306) 634-8610

Melfort Real Estate Board
c/o Century 21, PO Box 21
Melfort, SK S0E 1A0
Tel.: (306) 752-9316, Fax: (306) 752-3199

Moose Jaw Real Estate Board
79 Hochelaga Street West
Moose Jaw, SK S6H 2E9
Tel.: (306) 693-9544, Fax: (306) 692-4463
www.reginarealtors.com

Prince Albert Real Estate Board
218B South Industrial Drive
Prince Albert, SK S6V 7L8
Tel.: (306) 764-8755, Fax: (306) 763-0555
Email: **pareb@sk.sympatico.ca**
www.mls.ca/boards/princealbert

Swift Current Real Estate Association Inc
211- 12 Cheadle Street West
Swift Current, SK S9H 0A9
Tel.: (306) 773-4326, Fax: (306) 773-3917

The Saskatoon Real Estate Board
1149 - Eighth Street East
Saskatoon, SK S7H 0S3
Tel.: (306) 244-4453, Fax: (306) 343-1420
www.sreb.com

Weyburn Real Estate Board
1-33 5th Street
Weyburn, SK S4H 0Y9
Tel.: (306) 842-0300, Fax: (306) 842-5520

Yorkton Real Estate Association Inc.
40 - 41 Broadway West
Yorkton, SK S3N 0L6
Tel.: (306) 783-3067, Fax: (306) 786-3231

Yukon

Yukon Real Estate Association
PO Box 5292
Whitehorse, YK, Y1A 4Z2
Tel.: (867) 668-2070, Fax: (867) 668-2070
Email: **mail@yrea.yk.ca**
www.yrea.yk.ca

Appendix 3: How Much Does It Cost To Close?

The following chart shows average closing costs across Canada by province. In most cases, the prices listed represent averages and are examples only. However, they are still valuable as a means by which you can plan and budget accordingly.

"Home Closing Services" is a service provided by lawyers working in conjunction with title insurance company First Canadian Title (www.firstcanadiantitle.com). Included in the Home Closing Services costs shown are legal representation, disbursements you have to pay your lawyer, and the premium for title insurance policies protecting both the owner and lender.

"Mortgage insurance underwriting fee" is the cost to apply for a high ratio mortgage. Not included in this fee is the premium paid to a default insurer, which is added onto the amount borrowed and typically paid by the lender.

Other costs listed are registration costs (for the registration of all pertinent documents relating to the transaction) and transfer taxes, which are based on the value of the property purchased and paid to the local government upon closing. Of course, the fees associated with closing a real estate transaction vary by transaction. Other possible fees that are not listed in the cost comparison below include an appraisal fee, which is paid to validate that the home being purchased is worth what it costs.

How Much Does It Cost To Close?

Conditions:

Purchase Price $175,000.00

Mortgage Amount $133,000.00

	Home Closing Services price	Home Closing Services taxes	Registration Costs	Transfer Taxes	Average Mortgage Insurance Underwriting Fee	Tax on Mortgage Insurance Premium	TOTAL
Atlantic Provinces							
New Brunswick	$899.00	$104.85	$110.00	$437.50	$120.00	n/a	$1,671.35
Nova Scotia	$899.00	$104.85	$95.00	$2,625.00	$120.00	n/a	$3,843.85
Newfoundland	$999.00	$149.85	$908.10	n/a	$120.00	$249.38	$2,426.33
Prince Edward Island	$699.00	$34.93	$525.00	n/a	$120.00	n/a	$1,378.93
ONTARIO	$1,099.00	$78.93	$141.40	$1,475.00	$120.00	$133.00	$3,047.33
QUEBEC	$575.00	$77.51	$1,448.00	$1,500.00	$120.00	$149.63	$3,870.14
Western Provinces							
Alberta	$599.00	$33.60	$104.00	n/a	$120.00	n/a	$856.60
British Columbia	$619.00	$72.10	$110.00	$1,750.00	$120.00	n/a	$2,671.10
Manitoba	$539.00	$27.23	$120.00	$1,275.00	$120.00	n/a	$2,081.23
Saskatchewan	$599.00	$63.70	$368.00† $284.00††	n/a	$120.00	n/a	$1,434.70

† Transfer Registration Cost

†† Mortgage Registration Cost

Source: First Canadian Title

Glossary

The following terms represent key components in typical real estate transactions. This glossary has been adapted from material published by the Canadian Real Estate Association (reprinted with permission). You can find a comprehensive glossary on its Web site at **www.mls.ca/crea**.

Agreement of Purchase and Sale: The document through which the prospective buyer sets out the price and conditions under which he or she will buy the property.

Amortization: Paying off a debt, such as a mortgage, by installments. The conventional amortization period for a mortgage is anywhere between 15 and 25 years. The shorter the amortization period, the less interest you have to pay.

Appraisal: An estimate of a property's value.

Balanced Market: A balanced market exists when the supply of homes available for sale is just enough to meet the demands of those looking to purchase a home.

Beacon Score: A measure of credit worthiness.

Bridge Financing: An interim loan against the equity in a current home towards the purchase of a new home. Bridge financing is used to bridge the time gap between closing dates when the home that is being purchased closes before the home that is being sold.

Broker: A person licensed by the provincial or territorial government to trade in real estate. Real estate brokers may form companies or offices, which appoint sales representatives to provide services to the seller or buyer, or they may provide the same services themselves. In parts of Canada, brokers are referred to as agents.

Buyer Agency Agreement: A written agreement between the buyer and the buyer's agent, outlining the agency relationship between the two parties and the manner in which the buyer's agent will be compensated. In some provinces, a buyer agency relationship arises automatically, without a written agreement establishing the relationship.

Buyer's Agent: A person or firm representing the buyer. A buyer agent's primary allegiance is to the buyer. The buyer is the buyer agent's client.

Buyer's Market: A market in which the conditions are considered favourable to buyers. In a buyer's market, the supply of homes available for sale is greater than the demand for them.

Closing: The day the legal title to the property changes hands.

CMHC: Canada Mortgage and Housing Corporation. A Crown corporation providing information services and mortgage loan insurance.

Debt Service Ratio: The measurement of debt payments to gross household income which may include, in addition to the main wage earner's salary, salaries of other wage earners, commissions, bonuses, overtime, etc.

Equity: The difference between the value of the property and the amount owing (if any) on the mortgage.

Fair Market Value: A property value that is considered reasonable when compared with other properties on the market.

GE Capital Mortgage Insurance Company: The only private sector source of mortgage insurance to lenders in Canada.

Gross Debt Service: The amount of money needed to pay principal, interest, taxes, and sometimes energy costs. If the dwelling unit is a condominium, all or a portion of common fees are included, depending on what expenses are covered.

Gross Debt Service Ratio: Gross debt service divided by household income. A rule of thumb is that GDS should not exceed 30%. It is also referred to as PIT (principal, interest, and taxes) over income. Sometimes energy costs are added to the formula, producing PITE, which moves the rule of thumb GDS to 32%.

Interest Rate Differential: The difference between the rate on a mortgage and the current market rate, based on the outstanding balance on the mortgage and the amount remaining on the term.

Lien: An encumbrance on the title of a property.

Listing Agreement: The legal agreement between the listing broker and the seller, setting out the services to be rendered, describing the property for sale, and stating the terms of payment. A commission is generally payable to the broker upon closing.

Multiple Listing Service (MLS): A catalogue used in conjunction with a real estate database service, operated by local real estate boards, in which properties may be listed, purchased, or sold.

MLS Online: A Web site that posts property advertisements and consumer-related information supplied by individual real estate boards and associations across Canada.

Mortgage: A contract providing security for the repayment of a loan, registered against the property, with stated rights and remedies in the event of default. Lenders consider both the property (security) and the financial worth of the borrower (covenant) in deciding on a mortgage loan.

Mortgage Broker: A person or company having contacts with financial institutions or individuals wishing to invest in mortgages. The mortgagor pays the broker a fee for arranging the mortgage. Appraisal and legal services may or may not be included in the fee.

Mortgage Insurer: In Canada, high-ratio mortgages (those representing more than 75% of the property value) must be insured against default by either CMHC or private insurers. The borrower must arrange and pay for the insurance, which protects the lender against default.

Off Title Search: A search of utility, municipal government, and provincial government records. Typically done to determine whether a property complies with appropriate bylaws, to confirm payment status of various accounts such as property taxes and utility accounts, and to verify that no work orders are outstanding against a property.

Realtor: A title identifying real estate professionals in Canada who are members of The Canadian Real Estate Association and, as such, subscribe to a high standard of professional service and to a strict code of ethics.

Term: The actual life of a mortgage contract—from six months to ten years—at the end of which the mortgage becomes due and payable unless the lender renews the mortgage for another term (*see* Amortization).

Seller's Agent: The seller's agent represents the seller, either as a listing agent under the listing with the seller, or by cooperating as a sub-agent, typically through the MLS system. In dealing with prospective buyers (customers), the seller's agent can provide a variety of information and services to assist the buyer in his or her decision-making. The seller's agent does not represent the buyer.

Seller's Market: A market in which the conditions are considered favourable to sellers. In a seller's market, the demand for homes exceeds the supply.

Title: The bundle of rights associated with a property. Title proves ownership of the property.

Title Search: A search of the registered title to a property to determine, among other things, whether the seller has legal authority to convey ownership rights and to ensure that the property is free of encumbrances.

Endnotes

Chapter 1

1. Mario Fortin and Andre Leclerc, "Demographic Changes and Real Housing Prices in Canada," *CMHC Toronto Housing Outlook*, Nov. 2000.

2. David K. Foot with Daniel Stoffman, *Boom, Bust & Echo*, (Toronto: Macfarlane, Walter & Ross, 1996), 28.

3. Ibid., 35.

4. Glenn H Miller, Jr., "Demographic Influences on Household Growth and Housing Activity," *Economic Review* (Federal Reserve Bank of Kansas City, Sept/Oct 1988), 34-48.

5. David Weil and Gregory Mankiw, "The Baby Boom, The Baby Bust, and The Housing Market" *The Journal of Regional Science and Urban Economics* 19 (1989), 235-258.

6. "Clayton Housing Report," December 1999.

7. David Baxter, "The Myth of the Vanishing Purchaser: Demographics and the Future of Housing Demand in Canada," (Vancouver: Urban Futures Institute, 1997).

8. Mario Fortin and Andre Leclerc, "Demographic Changes and Real Housing Prices in Canada," (Ottawa: Canada Mortgage and Housing Corporation, October 1999).

9. Ibid., ii.

10. CMCH, Highlights from "Demographic Changes and Real Housing Prices in Canada," *Socio-economic Series* Issue 62, 2.

11. Derek Holt, "Special Report: The Impact of Retirement on Residential Property Markets" (Toronto: Royal Bank of Canada, October 1999).

12. Urban Futures Institute, "Help Wanted: Projections of Canada's Labour Force Over the Next Four Decades" (Vancouver: Urban Futures Institute, August 1999).

13. Statistics Canada chart, reproduced in Derek Holt, "Boom Echo Entering Housing Market — Canada" (Toronto: Royal Bank of Canada).

14. Derek Holt, "The Impact of Retirement."

15. Royal Bank of Canada, "8th Annual Home Ownership Survey" (February 2001).

16. Derek Holt, "The Impact of Retirement."

17. Quoted in Derek Holt, "The Impact of Retirement."

18. David Baxter, "Adding a Million: A Context for Change Management in the City of Toronto" (Vancouver: Urban Futures Institute, released March 2001).

19. Derek Holt, "The Impact of Retirement."

Chapter 2

1. "Housing as an Investment," jointly produced by Re/Max of Western Canada, Re/Max Ontario-Atlantic and Will Dunning Inc. (Mississauga, January 2001).

2. "Royal Lepage National Home Attitude Poll Spring 2001": Canadians rank April (22%), May (21%), and June (18%) as the best times to sell and December (11%) and January (11%) as the best times to buy.

3. The National Association of Home Builders, "The Next Decade for Housing" (2001).

4. Will Dunning, quoted in *REM* (January 2001), 42.

5. CMHC, "Consumer Intentions To Buy or Renovate: A Home Survey" (Ottawa, 2001).

6. Clayton research based on data obtained from The Canadian Real Estate Association and local boards.

7. CMHC, "CMHC Housing Outlook First Quarter 2001."

8. "Robust Sales Activity Continues in Housing Market and Causes Prices to Increase Year over Year" on Royal Lepage Web site (**www.royallepage.ca**), April 3, 2001.

9. CMHC, "Consumer Intention To Buy or Renovate."

10. City of Toronto Web site (**www.city.Toronto.on.ca**), Ward Profiles/Total Assessment and Total Tax Change, Ward Comparison by Property Class.

11. U.S. National Association of Realtors, 2001.

12. HomeGain online survey, November 2000, as reported in *Inman News Features*, Monday, December 18, 2000.

13. American Society of Home Inspectors and National Association of Realtors, 2001, as reported in *Inman News Features*, March 30, 2001.

14. As reported in *Inman News Features*, Wednesday, April 11, 2001.

Chapter 3

1. U.S. National Association of Realtors, as reported in *Inman News Features*, October 29, 2001.

2. National Association of Realtors, "Profile of Home Buyers and Sellers, 2000."

3. "2001 National Home Attitude Poll" by Core Strategies for Royal Lepage Real Estate Services Ltd.

4. National Association of Realtors.

5. National Association of Realtors.

Chapter 4

1. CMHC, "National Housing Outlook Third Quarter 2001."

2. CMHC, "Building," August and September 1996.

3. Remodeling Online/Hanley-Wood National Averages 2000-2001, "Cost vs. Value Report."

4. National Association of Realtors Web site, **www.nar.realtor.com**.

5. Appraisal Institute of Canada, Press Release September 1999 on their Web site, **www.aicanada.org**.

6. Canadian Home Builders' Association, "Renovationg Your Home, Ideas, Plans and Budgets, Lifestyle Renovations," **www.chba.ca/renovatingyourhome/ ideasplansbudgets/lifestylrenovations.html**.

7. The example used to illustrate this second scenario comes from David Karas, President of Money Concepts (an established Canadian financial planning firm).

Chapter 5

1. Overseas Private Investment Corporation (**www.opic.gov** report), "Bridging The Housing Gap in Emerging Markets," Fall 2000.

2. Royal Lepage press release, "Increasing Number of Canadians Embracing Technology in Residential Real Estate Process" (Toronto, February 28, 2001): The results of a survey conducted by Core Strategies Inc. showed that more than 72% of 1,000 Canadians surveyed plan to use the Internet in their next real estate transaction.

3. Joint survey of CMHC and CIMBL (Canadian Institute of Mortgage Brokers and Lenders), "Fall 2001 Annual Survey."

4. Ibid.

5. Ibid.

6. Dr. Moshe Milevsky, PhD, "Study for Manulife Financial" (Toronto, April 2000).

7. Canada Customs and Revenue Agency (CCRA), Carrying Charges and Interest Expense (line 221).

8. Peter Norman, "A Homeowner's Guide to Interest Rates and Economic Conditions — Dec. 1997" (Toronto: Clayton Research, 1997).

9. Ibid.

Index